Let Us Serve Them All Their Days

Younger Volunteers Serving Homebound Elderly Persons

Written and edited by Larry Couch

A publication of
The National Council on the Aging
409 Third Street, SW
Washington, DC 20024

THE RESOURCE CENTER
ETR Associates
4 Carbonero Way
Scotts Valley, CA 95066
1-800-860-2684

DATE DUE

Let Us Serve Them All Their Days: Your Volunteers Serving Homebound Elderly Persons
Couch, Larry
R3342

DATE	ISSUED TO	
12/21/10	C. Borden	1/11/11

National Service Resource Center
ETR Associates
4 Carbonero Way
Scotts Valley, CA 95066

GAYLORD M2G

TABLE OF CONTENTS

Introduction	1
Lessons learned	5
Successful project elements	11
How to initiate and expand intergenerational projects	15
A case study report	21
Index to project profiles	35
Project profiles	
Help/maintenance projects	41
Meal delivery projects	69
Home service projects	81
Telephone reassurance projects	129
Other service projects	137
Other perspectives on intergenerational projects	153
Resource guide	159
Summary	167

Introduction

The dream of the intergenerational movement is to bring together the elderly, who need a friend, with the young, who need a sense of purpose. By reaching out to older people in our communities, we give younger people a place to be of service.

This is a "how to" book. If you are interested in beginning an intergenerational project where young people volunteer to work with the frail, homebound elderly, this book is offered as a guide. We present examples of highly successful projects, the lessons we learned from those projects, the elements needed for a successful project, and a step-by-step approach for initiating new projects. We also present profiles of selected projects with the names and phone numbers of project directors. In addition, we invited leaders in the field of intergenerational projects to present their view on initiating and expanding projects.

We hope that this is more than a "how to" book. Intergenerational projects are desperately needed in communities across the United States to meet the needs of both older and younger persons. For those who have never considered starting a project, we hope to convey a sense of what is possible and an appreciation of what is being done. For those who are already involved, we hope this will be a place to meet old friends and an opportunity to make new ones. And for those who have considered starting a project but have hesitated, we hope to make confident the wavering and make bold the cautious.

In October 1989, NCOA received a grant from the Wallerstein Foundation for Geriatric Life Improvement to assess a selected number of projects that offer youth volunteer services for homebound frail elderly persons. We completed a mail survey and identified hundreds of organizations that sponsor youth projects serving this population. After carefully screening the responses, we identified projects that appeared unique in approach and effectiveness. Our criteria were that the projects should have been in existence for at least two years, involve a significant number of volunteers and elderly, and embody an unique approach. The last criterion was the most important. We also looked for a broad geographic distribution.

All across the country, we found that young people are helping the frail homebound elderly. They deliver food, shovel snow from walks, install banisters, cut down trees for firewood, take elderly persons for walks, go shopping with them. Most importantly, they sit and talk with elderly persons, listening to the stories of childhoods in distant countries, learning how it feels to lose a loved one, and finding out what it was like to fight in World War I.

We learned about a young man in New York City who helps an elderly man down a flight of stairs to go for a walk in the park. Because of that young person, an older man will feel the warmth of sunlight and see trees and the sky. Through physical infirmity, the older man is trapped in his apartment day after day. But he rediscovers the world because a younger person has volunteered his time. The newspapers won't report the event, the television stations will not broadcast it. Yet, the event is of importance. It is certainly important to the older man, and also to the younger man. The older man again experiences a sense of freedom, and the younger man learns that he has something of value to offer the world. They both shed their sense of alienation and discover they are connected to each other and, through each other, to everyone else in the world.

During this review, we learned that project directors and staff were invariably interested in projects in other parts of the country. This book is an attempt to address this issue. The projects selected are not necessarily the best. However, they are all successful, and they all reflect a sense of commitment and dedication on the part of the young to serve those in need. The Wallerstein Foundation for Geriatric Life Improvement generously offered NCOA funds to publish our findings.

We did not limit the projects to those which recruit exclusively younger volunteers. Many projects involve volunteers of all ages. Two of the projects described under "Other service projects," focus primarily on seeking older volunteers to serve the homebound elderly. When initiating your project, you may want to focus your recruiting efforts on elderly persons, or create a project that includes both older and younger volunteers.

In completing our survey, we were honored to meet with some of the leaders in the field of intergenerational programs. Many of them were early pioneers in the field and have had years of experience in developing and administering programs. We asked several of them to write an essay on why they believe intergenerational programs are important, on what they have learned from their involvement with these programs, on how younger and older persons benefit from these programs, or on some other topic of their choosing. Following the abstracts on selected projects, we present excerpts from their essays. We believe that you will find their comments informational, insightful, and, hopefully, motivational.

Larry Couch
Editor

Lessons Learned

Let Us Serve Them All Their Days • 5

Reviewing these projects brought to light a number of lessons about what it takes to establish a project with young volunteers helping frail older people—information, ideas, resources, techniques—to make a project work. For example, when you plan your project, you should consider the audience, the services, project site, staff, and mobilization of resources.

Here are some general questions to guide you in making decisions about your project.

- Who are the people that you are trying to reach?

- What services do you want to provide?

- Are the anticipated benefits primarily for the young volunteers or for elderly persons?

- If for elderly persons, will your approach be primarily person-to-person or will it be a community-wide approach?

- What resources do you have available?

- Can you identify persons who have had experience in initiating, maintaining, or expanding the type of project you wish to start?

- How will you motivate persons to become volunteers?

- Will it be a school-based project?

- Who will you choose for your coordinator?

- How will you fund the project?

- Do you plan to link with other agencies and institutions?

- Will you focus on homebound persons or persons in hospitals and nursing homes?

- Will this be a short-term or long-term project?

- How will you evaluate the success of your project?

- What experience has your community had with intergenerational projects?

Let Us Serve Them All Their Days • 7

If you are planning a person-to-person, or "friendly visiting" project, here are some issues which you will need to resolve.

- What type of transportation will be available for the volunteers? If using their own vehicles, will they be reimbursed for mileage?

- What type of insurance coverage will you require?

- How will you decide on the matching of volunteers with the persons they will serve?

- Will the volunteers visit the elderly person alone or as a team of two or more volunteers?

- If it is a school-based project, how will you select volunteers; what criteria will you use; what sort of mix will you develop?

- What type of training will you provide the volunteers?

- Will the training prepare the volunteer to act as an advocate for the elderly person?

- How will you prepare the volunteers for the possibility that their elderly friend may die?

- What types of services will be provided?

- Who will cover the costs for the materials?

- Will a nominal cost be charged for the services?

- If demand exceeds services available, what criteria will you use in determining who will receive the services?

- Have you considered approaching an organization, such as a school, fraternity, or sorority, and requesting that they take on a particular project to benefit elderly persons?

Are you considering special activities which require detailed planning and preparation? You should look at these four areas.

- What types of outings are being considered? A senior prom? A special Christmas dinner? A visit to the county fair?

- Will the same participants be selected each year, or will the project seek to involve different participants?

- How will you develop, advertise, and implement the project?

- How will you modify or expand the project, or replicate the project elsewhere?

Regardless of the type of project that you elect to start, the most important question is: Who will you choose as the coordinator? The success or failure of a project very often depends on the person chosen to monitor and guide the project. The most important quality to look for in a coordinator is reliability. Can the person be trusted to do what he or she promises to do? Without this quality, the project will never succeed.

Although it is not always possible to find a charismatic leader, it is important—especially at the junior high and high school level—to include students who are popular and respected by their fellow students. The intergenerational project should be seen as an "in" activity. To the extent possible, being a volunteer should be given prestige status—an honor to be sought.

Do not be concerned about the number of volunteers or the number of elderly persons served. Concentrate on maintaining a positive, upbeat attitude regarding the project. Never complain to the volunteers that more people are not volunteering or that the project isn't reaching as many elderly as originally anticipated. Celebrate small successes and recognize everyday triumphs. If an older person is able to maintain his or her independence for an additional six months because of the work of a volunteer, you have cause to congratulate the volunteer and yourself. If one roof is repaired, consider all your efforts worthwhile.

Successful Project Elements

Let Us Serve Them All Their Days • 11

What are the elements needed for a successful project? Through our assessment, we have identified the following.

The most important element in any successful intergenerational project is the Project Coordinator. He or she must be able to elicit the trust and respect of the volunteers. The Project Director must be reliable and committed to the program. Without such a person, no program can function. With such a person, miracles can occur.

In NCOA's nationwide survey, we found many situations where the program developed and grew simply because of the commitment of a person who not only initiated the project but also served as the project coordinator. In Texas, a social work student saw the need for friendly visiting and chore service for elderly persons and started a community-wide project. In Maryland, an assistant high school principal began and coordinated a project because he saw a need to involve his students more with the community. Time and again, we saw projects started, maintained, and expanded because of one person's belief and dedication.

The second most important element in establishing and maintaining an intergenerational program is a project site: office space, telephone, and supplies. The volunteers need a place where they can give and receive information. Without a site, the effort will not have a focus and will not gain the needed attention and momentum. Volunteers will not have a sense of belonging and will lose interest. Persons who might be interested and willing to volunteer will probably not know of the program.

In addition, the site not only provides the space but is also the physical evidence of the commitment to maintain and expand the program. Ideally, this site will also have enough space for the volunteers to meet regularly for the purpose of exchanging ideas and sharing feelings. It also provides the Project Director the necessary logistics for maintaining public relations and recruitment of new volunteers.

The third most important element is training. Although many programs function using the existing knowledge and skills of the volunteers, or rely on on-the-job training, formal training is recommended to ensure that the volunteers have the basic knowledge and skills needed. Training is also needed to enrich and deepen the knowledge and skills of the volunteers and to help the volunteers incorporate, understand, and benefit from their experiences.

Although friendly visiting is simple in concept, the human dynamics can be complex. Experience has shown that the volunteer should receive both initial and ongoing training. Prior to the first visit, he or she should be given at least four to six hours of training in the aging process, communication, and what to do in an emergency.

Discussion of the aging process should include a discussion of myths and facts concerning older people, and a discussion of attitudes toward the aging process. Techniques for improving communication should be presented, such as the importance of good eye contact, an open body posture (uncrossed legs and arms), leaning forward slightly, and asking follow-up questions that are non-intrusive.

Training on how to handle a crisis situation may include teaching the Heimlich maneuver in case of choking, along with instruction on how to provide for persons with special needs. Discuss the kinds of emergencies that may arise and what actions are appropriate for each emergency. Each volunteer should have emergency phone numbers in case of a crisis.

Volunteers should receive in-service training of at least two hours each month. This training may include discussion on food and nutrition, and health and financial issues facing elderly persons. Training may also be provided on how to act as an advocate for elderly persons when they apply for benefits from government and social service agencies.

Monthly in-service training provides an excellent opportunity for the volunteers to share their experiences. They should be encouraged to talk with each other, and the Project Coordinator, about issues that have surfaced during their volunteer work. The monthly meeting can help create a relationship among the volunteers and offer each volunteer feedback from other volunteers about problems and concerns.

In training, mistakes and false assumptions by the volunteer can be unmasked early on—and a deeper, more joyful experience provided to both the volunteer and the elderly person. Without structured training, learning can be a slow and painful process. Since the volunteer is not receiving any monetary reward, he or she may well resign rather than undergo this process. As a society, we tend not to value those occupations that do not pay well—and assume that if an occupation does not pay well, then few skills are involved. Since the volunteers receive little or no remuneration, the unspoken assumption is that no skills are involved.

But whenever one person seriously becomes involved in the life of another person, a great deal of knowledge and skill are involved. Appropriate training will emphasize that the volunteer must understand the limits of his or her role and the needs and expectations of the clients; have a certain amount of self-knowledge, self-understanding, and self-acceptance in order to be of value and not be emotionally needy; and learn not to place unrealistic expectations and demands on the other person. In addition, specific skill—such as technical or trade skill—may be required by the nature of the volunteer work.

The fourth most important element is—especially in rural areas—transportation. While volunteers do not seek to gain monetary reward for their work, many do not have the financial resources to spend for transportation and other expenses. Unless the program seeks to involve as volunteers only the financially fortunate, consideration should be given to reimbursing costs associated with the volunteer work. A modest stipend will greatly expand the pool of persons able to offer services.

The fifth most important element is recognition and award ceremonies. Everyone needs to hear "thank you." A public "thank you" will go a long way in maintaining existing volunteers and recruiting new volunteers. The ceremonies are also an important educational tool for informing the community of the program and the services that the program offers. During the ceremonies, staff, volunteers, and elderly persons have an opportunity to review their accomplishments, express their appreciation to each other, and look forward to future visits and activities.

How to Initiate and Expand Intergenerational Projects

Let Us Serve Them All Their Days • 15

Having reviewed the questions based on the lessons learned from successful projects, and the elements needed for a successful project, you are now ready to begin a step-by-step approach to developing your project.

1. Conduct an informal needs assessment. Review the questions, and your answers, from "Lessons Learned." Find out if there is interest in your community for a friendly visiting project, a home repair project, or another type of intergenerational project.

    A "needs assessment" may sound formidable, but it isn't. Talk with various community leaders such as senior center directors, pastors and rabbis, principals and teachers, social service agency directors and their staff, and members of youth and senior organizations. Talk with your younger and older friends. Ask them what is being done and what, in their opinion, needs to be done.

    At least initially, you are not seeking statistics. All you are searching for is a general idea of what projects exist in your community, what organizations are involved with these projects, a sense of some of the unmet needs, and the likelihood of recruiting volunteers to help meet those needs.

2. Form an advisory committee. Committee members are an excellent source for suggestions, ideas, publicity, recruitment, moral support, and fund-raising.

    Keep it simple. At this time, do not be concerned about organizational structures or by-laws. All you want is a group of people who are willing to meet on a regular basis and share their ideas and opinions.

    Try to involve people with a variety of skills and experiences. If possible, seek out people who have been involved with intergenerational projects. Look for people associated with senior and youth organizations.

3. Develop a written plan of action.

    A. Write a mission statement. In the statement, give the overarching reason why you are embarking on this endeavor. A mission statement could be "To engage the young people in our community to ensure that every elderly person has safe and adequate housing." Don't worry as to whether or not you can accomplish it. The mission statement comes from the heart. It should inspire you and others. During discouraging times, it should serve to remind you of the importance of what you are doing and keep you on track.

        Be sure to write it down. By developing a written mission statement, your advisory committee can clearly state the nature of their purpose. Make the mission statement public. Some groups include it on their letterhead. However you decide to do it, make your mission statement public and visible.

Let Us Serve Them All Their Days • 17

B. Set goals: State what you would like to accomplish, such as "Start a friendly visiting project for the homebound using high school students." Or, "Start a home repair project serving elderly persons and involving young people who have dropped out of school."

Select your goals carefully. Are they feasible? Do they have wide support among your committee members? Although you can always change your goals, you are in danger of losing valuable time, energy, commitment, and credibility. And be modest. Unrealistic goals can only breed failure and discouragement.

C. Set objectives: Describe specifically, in measurable terms, what you hope to achieve. An objective would be, "During the next 12 months, recruit 15 high school students to be matched with 15 frail, homebound elderly."

D. List specific activities or tasks to accomplish each objective. For example:

   i.   Get in touch with the principal at Middlevale High School and seek her support for the project.

   ii. Identify a teacher who is supportive of the project and ask him or her to help coordinate the project.

   iii. Meet with students and explain the project.

   iv. Provide four hours of training to the students.

4. Develop a budget to help monitor revenues and expenses. The budget should consist of an income budget—how much money do you have available, and an expense budget—what are your expenses. If financial management is not your strong point, try to involve a person with that strength on your committee.

   Each community, depending upon its needs and resources, must define the ideal or model budget for an intergenerational program. However, a consideration of these five elements may be useful in arriving at a workable budget.

   A budget designed for a moderate size project of approximately thirty volunteers—for either a rural or an urban community—might consist of the following expenses.

Salary plus fringe for full-time project coordinator	$30,000
Office space, telephone, office supplies, etc.	15,000
Training and supplies	5,000
Transportation and other reimbursable costs	4,000
Recognition dinners and awards	1,000
Total	**$55,000**

5. Conduct a fund-raising campaign. Funds may be sought from institutions, such as schools and social service agencies, and from individuals. Funds may be raised from community events such as fairs, luncheons, dinners, and special events. Advisory committee members with experience in raising funds can be of invaluable assistance.

    The lack of an effective fund-raising campaign is perhaps the main reason for project failures. Start the campaign as soon as possible and never stop. If you wait until three months before you are out of funds, it's too late. Begin now.

6. Use public relations and publicity. Speak up and let people know what you are doing. Use the local newspaper and other media. Get a camera and take pictures of the volunteers working with elderly persons. (Be sure to get written permission from those photographed before releasing the photos for publication.)

    Newspapers and local radio and TV stations are always looking for human interest stories. They want to know what you are doing. You have to present the information to them in an interesting manner. If you had a committee meeting, what issues were discussed? What decisions made? What successes were reported?

    Get to know some of the reporters. Keep them informed. If you don't get coverage, find out why. Look for ways to develop a good story. For example, interview one of your volunteers and tell how he or she got involved and what his or her experiences have been. Interview a frail, elderly person and learn his or her story. Of course, always get written permission from the person before submitting the article for publication.

    Make getting articles published one of your objectives, as in "Submit an article each month to the Post Tribune." If people read and see favorable stories about your efforts on a regular basis, you will have gone a long ways toward accomplishing your goals and strengthening your organization.

7. Organize a brainstorming session. If you have an ongoing project but have not initiated new services recently, and you see needs that are not being met, you may wish to conduct a brainstorming session. Invite members of your staff and advisory committee, your volunteers, and elderly persons in your community for an informal gathering. Urge people to suggest new endeavors, new ways of doing things. At this stage, don't worry about how you are going to pay for it. Simply get the ideas out.

    Tack some butcher paper on a wall and start listing the ideas. Make it a rule of the game that no one squelches an idea. Have a prohibition against anyone saying "That can't be done," or "We would never be able to afford to do that," or "We tried that before and it doesn't work."

    In a subsequent meeting, review the ideas, select the ideas that appear to be the most feasible, and start the difficult process of transforming the ideas into reality. Be ready for failures and setbacks, but expect success. Get enthusiastic about your new endeavors, and let your enthusiasm be contagious. Remember the importance of your mission and the needs of the elderly persons in your community. You're bound to succeed.

And now, let's take a look at what is happening around the country. These models should help you decide what direction you want to take.

A Case Study Report

Let Us Serve Them All Their Days • 21

In our research and assessment, we identified four main project categories:

a. Person-to-person or "friendly visiting" projects involve young people visiting the frail elderly in their homes.

b. Young persons provide services for elderly persons. In these projects, rendering services is the primary purpose of the visit, with "friendly visiting" as a secondary purpose. Services may be as simple as mowing the yard, or as extensive as putting a new roof on the house.

c. Elderly persons are given an opportunity to leave their homes for special "outings" or "vacations."

d. Young persons advocate for institutional change within the community to benefit the frail, homebound elderly.

Although most projects overlapped in services, they can generally be classified within these categories.

Person-to-person or "friendly visiting" projects

• The Adopt-A-Grandparent (AAG) project is sponsored by the University of Vermont at Burlington. The project is part of the Volunteers in Action (VIA) project, which offers the students a wide range of volunteer opportunities—from short-term commitments of a few months to long-term commitments that last a year or two.

AAG matches college students with frail, homebound elderly. The elderly person becomes the "grandfather" or "grandmother." When a volunteer speaks of her "grandfather," he is a "real" grandfather to her, even though they are not related.

The use of the terms "grandfather" and "grandmother" is not something added on but rather reflects the central idea and motivating force behind the project. Adopt-A-Grandparent means what it says. The older person becomes a grandparent for the student and the student relates to the older person as a grandparent. Frequently students volunteer for the AAG programs because they have sensed the absence of a grandfather or grandmother in their lives. And in return, the older person tends to relate to the student as an absent grandchild, or a grandchild they never had.

Max Soble, a Jewish immigrant, fled Russia in 1918. In the midst of the Revolution, he saw the murder of his 17-year old friend who had lived next door. Without family or friends, he lived day to day, not knowing where he would sleep the next night. Eventually he reached Poland, where he lived for several years. Unable to get a work permit, he lived hand-to-mouth. In 1934, he was finally able to immigrate to the United States.

Settling in the small Jewish community in Burlington, Mr. Soble did not marry until late in life. He chose not to have children. Emotionally scarred by the events of his own youth, he feared to have children who would grow up only to die of hunger or in war.

Mr. Soble is ninety years old and is fully alert and alive. He has a positive glow about him. Somehow, despite all the adversity he has lived through, he has kept his youthful vigor and vitality. When asked, he credits his happiness to the visits of his "granddaughter." Kim has been visiting him regularly for about two years and has a deep affection for him.

Apparently, the relationship with his "granddaughter" has been very important to his emotional health. A social worker from the Visiting Nurse Association mentioned that Mr. Soble had previously had periods of deep depression. For example, Mr. Soble is concerned that since Kim is in her senior year, she will be leaving the university. However, she will be living near Burlington and they are making plans for staying in touch. Also, AAG will seek another volunteer to succeed Kim.

A volunteer's leaving may often be a hardship for the older person; however, the project coordinator believes that most elderly people have learned the difficult lesson of letting go and forming new bonds of affection. Every relationship eventually ends, and so will the relationships formed within the AAG project. What is important is that, for a number of months or years, a student has a grandparent and an elderly person has a grandchild.

- A variation on "friendly visiting" is the project in Edgewood, Maryland, about 30 miles north of Baltimore. Although close to the urban centers of both Baltimore and Washington, D.C., Edgewood is very much a poor, rural community. William Hallock, Assistant Principal of the Edgewood Middle School, initiated the project. At the time, he was concerned not primarily about the frail, homebound elderly but about some of his seventh and eighth grade students who were doing poorly in school, who were drifting, and who had an "attitude."

He started the project a few years ago, with the students visiting elderly persons in their homes, doing simple chores. Mr. Hallock is delighted by the results. The attendance card of one of the students showed frequent absences and tardiness. Citations were also shown for talking back and showing disrespect to her teachers. Then she became involved in the intergenerational project. Within a month, her attendance card showed no absences, no tardiness, and no citations for disrespect. This was not an isolated example. Overall, the students in the project improved their academic performance and their behavior. Mr. Hallock had wisely mixed honor students with the students-at-risk, but it is the students-at-risk that he is primarily tracking. In his view, the project is working.

- Youth in Service to the Elderly (YISTE), Pittsburgh, Pennsylvania, focuses on a one-to-one relationship between younger and older persons. Volunteers visit with elderly persons in nursing homes, in rehabilitation centers, and in their homes. YISTE is part of a larger intergenerational effort, Generations Together. Although begun as a private nonprofit organization, Generations Together is now an official unit of the University of Pittsburgh, under the umbrella of the University Center for Social and Urban Research.

Sitting in his wheelchair, Mr. Johnson had a thin, gaunt look about him. His volunteer, Yvonne, had mentioned that he was known to make off-color remarks to his female volunteers. When we entered his room, he had his back to the window. Yvonne asked him several conversational questions concerning his health. He seemed pleased by her attention but also annoyed. Yvonne is only 17. Some of the other volunteers hadn't shown up that day and, in addition to her regular visits, she was trying to cover for the others. She was feeling the pressure.

With each question that Yvonne asked, she pointed her finger at him. Suddenly he said, "Will you stop doing that. I feel like you are pointing a gun at me." Flustered, Yvonne mumbled an apology and rose to leave. As she was leaving, he wanted to know when she would return—he seemed afraid that he had offended her and that she might not come back. She assured him that she would be seeing him later.

Why did Yvonne sign up as a volunteer? She said, "I wanted to strengthen my resume to help me get into college." What was it about volunteer work that she liked? "I like it when I am able to get someone to smile."

Yvonne mentioned to us that she found going from room to room in the nursing home very stressful. She said it was easier when she assisted at some group activity. At 17, Yvonne was learning about herself and about the world. The director of the program keeps in touch with the volunteers on a regular basis to help them deal with the pressures involved in volunteer work.

Hooman is a 17-year old boy from Iran. He was just starting his volunteer work and was thoroughly enjoying it. Recently arrived in this country, he had spent two years in Germany. He said he was volunteering in order to get to know more people. He seemed relaxed and ready for whatever would happen next. Yvonne told him that she had arranged for him to visit an elderly lady who was known to be rather withdrawn. She thought the woman might relate to him since he spoke some German and the woman would be delighted to converse with Hooman in her native tongue. Hooman was pleased that he would be able to practice his German. New to this country, Hooman was as isolated as many of the residents in the rehabilitation center. Being imaginative and energetic, he had found a way to break through his own sense of isolation and, while doing so, to help others to break out of their isolation.

Tammy is a volunteer for home visiting under YISTE. We met with her in the apartment of her elderly friend, Mrs. Barsky. The apartment was furnished with an old-fashioned couch and chairs. On the wall hung photographs of friends and relatives, many of whom had passed away or moved to a distant city. Tammy and Mrs. Barsky get along fabulously. In the friendly give and take between them, any notion of "volunteer' and "client" quickly gets lost. What do they enjoy doing together? "Shopping." They were obviously having a great time, learning about each other and doing things together they both enjoy. Mrs. Barsky mentioned that Tammy was her fifth "volunteer." But she quickly added that Tammy was her favorite.

YISTE is expanding to serve elderly persons living in high-rise apartment buildings. Although able to live alone, many elderly persons suffer from isolation and loneliness. YISTE is working with local high schools to establish volunteer programs and to recruit volunteers to meet with elderly persons living in these apartments. The project is also attempting to recruit more student volunteers from the University of Pittsburgh.

• The Landon School, a private school located in Bethesda, Maryland, is affiliated with Iona House of Washington, D.C. Iona House is a private, nonprofit social service and information center for older people. The students visit elderly, low-income residents in the District. The students learn about older persons, about poverty, and about the value of volunteer work. They are learning how they feel about themselves when they do grocery shopping, change a light bulb, or perform some other small chore.

The program has been in existence for 10 years—largely because of the effort of one woman who became aware of the need for a volunteer program when her mother grew older and needed help. She decided to test her idea for a volunteer program at the Landon School. While she was organizing the program, she caught a student, who was bright, articulate and popular, doing something for which he could be expelled. She made an agreement with him— if he worked with her to help organize the volunteer program, she wouldn't tell. He agreed, and since then the program has witnessed a decade of success. The fact that the Landon School is an all boys' school is of particular interest because many schools have difficulty in recruiting young men for volunteer work.

Younger persons provide services for older persons

• CHIPPS (Community & Home Injury Prevention Project for Seniors) is sponsored by the San Francisco Department of Public Health. In cooperation with the San Francisco Conservation Corps, minor home repairs are provided free of charge to the frail elderly.

Too frequently the following scenario occurs. An elderly person living alone gets out of the bath, slips and falls, and is taken to the hospital with a broken hip. His relatives worry about his safety and are concerned that he may not be able to continue to live alone. After his hospital stay, he is taken to a nursing home. His days of independent living are over. All too frequently, his desire to continue to live also ends.

Meanwhile a young person may have dropped out of high school. He has trouble at home. Drifting from job to job, he has difficulty finding a career. He has not succeeded at school, and he is not succeeding in the field of work. He feels badly about himself. His only escape is drugs and alcohol. One night he gets into trouble with the law. Facing jail time and not yet 20, his life is coming to a dead end. With little on no self-esteem, he defines himself as a failure.

CHIPPS has found a way to transform these bleak realities. A common belief is that falls are inevitable for an older person. This is not true. Through minor home repairs, an older person's home can be made safe—preventing such accidents. The CHIPPS project enlists San Francisco Conservation Corpsmembers to make minor repairs and improvements, such as tacking down loose carpets, repairing light fixtures, installing grip bars in showers and on bathtubs, putting in banisters along steps, and repairing broken steps.

These repairs are minor, but they prevent major falls. Getting out of the bath one morning, an older man slips but is able to catch himself by grabbing hold of the grip bar. Because her carpet has been tacked down, an older woman does not trip and fall when she hurries across the room to answer the phone. Preventing the falls prevents the injuries. In a safe place, the frail elderly person is able to maintain independence.

CHIPPS also changes the scenario for younger persons. Instead of drifting, the young person is trained to do minor home repairs. They learn to install grip bars, put in banisters, repair light fixtures, fix broken steps. They learn that they have something important to offer society. Their self-esteem improves.

One corpsmember mentioned how pleased the older people are to have their homes repaired. Overall, the corpsmembers were very positive about their work. They knew they were being given another chance.

The corpsmembers are learning how to report to work on time and how to conduct themselves in a work situation, learning marketable skills, being paid a minimum salary, and, for some, doing court-ordered community work. They are learning how to be of service to society, and how much they have to offer society. This is the heart of voluntarism—people learning they have value and that they have something to offer to other people.

• In Austin, Texas, a group of volunteers known as the Austin Caregivers provides both friendly visiting and minor home repair. Gladys Azar, a woman in her late seventies, comes from Lebanon. She lives alone and subsists entirely on her Social Security check. She is an artist who works in several media, including charcoal, watercolors, oil, embroidery, and ceramics. Ms. Esparza is the volunteer working with Ms. Azar.

Ms. Azar's wooden house is in great need of repair and has been repeatedly burglarized. Ms. Esparza's husband came one day and painted the front of the house. He could not afford to paint the entire house, but he hoped that with the front painted, the house would look more "lived in" and less a prey for burglars.

Each time Ms. Azar realized she had been burglarized, she felt terrified that the burglar might still be in the house. The last time she was burglarized, she called Ms. Esparza, who came over and spent several hours with her. Ms. Azar has boarded up many of her windows in an effort to increase her security.

Paula Johnson, Special Projects Coordinator for the Texas Department on Aging, stated that community funds were frequently not available to fix up Ms. Azar's house, repair the plumbing, or to make it safe. Part of the problem is that Texas allocates very little money for social services. Ms. Johnson said that, of the 50 states, Texas is 47th in terms of expenditures for social service. The waiting time for weatherization can be four to five years. Many elderly may not live long enough to receive the services.

Ms. Esparza initially volunteered to visit with Ms. Azar for a six-month period. Three years later, Ms. Esparza is still visiting with Ms. Azar. Ms. Esparza said, "When you start caring for someone, you can't just stop caring. You can't put a time limit on loving someone."

• In Bryan, Texas, the Elder Aid project provides friendly visiting and minor and major home repair. Friendly visiting includes reading mail, an important service for many elderly who suffer from poor vision. Fifty college students put a new roof on Mrs. Ethel Nutcall's home. She said, "Before, when it rained, the water would just pour in." Now, with a new roof, her house stays warm and dry.

Mrs. Nutcall's home is in the midst of a small community of similar houses. Many of the houses appeared to need substantial repair. Although Mrs. Nutcall was fortunate in having her roof repaired, the project exemplified the strengths and limitations of a volunteer effort. Mrs. Nutcall's problem had been solved, but the larger problem of dilapidated and inadequate housing remains.

• Also in Bryan, the local Community Action Agency sponsors a Meals on Wheels program. Many of the meals are delivered by student volunteers. Although the clients live many miles apart, the meals are delivered on a regular basis, even during bad weather when the back roads are slippery and dangerous.

In spite of these difficulties, the program has been successful in soliciting six student volunteers from the local university. Each of these students serves meals to 20 elderly persons one day a week. They not only deliver the meals, they also check on the well-being of the clients. Each student volunteers for a semester. The use of volunteers makes it possible to serve more low-income elderly, many of whom may otherwise go hungry.

Elderly persons are given an opportunity to leave their homes for special "outings" or "vacations."

• The Little Brothers—Friends of the Elderly (also known as the Little Brothers of the Poor) originated in France in 1946 under the leadership of Armand Marquiset, a French nobleman. Marquiset, disturbed by the plight of elderly poor persons in Paris, left his wealthy surroundings and moved into one of the poorest areas of the city. He began taking food to the forgotten elderly.

From the beginning, the guiding motto of the Little Brothers was: "Flowers Before Bread." Marquiset believed that the poor elderly were entitled not only to the bare necessities of life, but also to luxuries. An elderly couple celebrating their wedding anniversary would be invited to a chateau crowded with guests and served a feast with flowers and champagne. The wife, who may never have had a wedding ring, would be presented with a diamond ring.

In France, the Little Brothers is now one of the major charity organizations. They maintain their "Flowers Before Bread" philosophy, recently taking 50 disabled elderly persons on a two-week luxury cruise along the Seine. In addition to France and the United States, Little Brothers has affiliates in Spain, Morocco, Canada, Ireland, and Mexico.

Little Brothers expanded its operation to the United States in 1959, establishing a site in one of Chicago's poorest neighborhoods. As Marquiset had done in Paris, Little Brothers began calling on the forgotten elderly, bringing them food and friendship. When asked how the philosophy of "Flowers Before Bread" translates into the everyday harsh reality of reaching out to the frail, homebound elderly, Little Brothers have a one-word answer: Friendship. By approaching an elderly persons as an "old friend," the Little Brothers hope to establish a relationship that is based on friendship, not simply on need.

For friends, people are willing to do more than provide the bare necessities. If an elderly person needs medical attention, a Little Brothers volunteer does more than simply provide transportation. The volunteer talks with the elderly person about his fears, waits for him at the doctor's office, helps him to get his prescription—in short, the volunteer does everything for that person that someone would do for a friend.

The organization has maintained its philosophy of "Flowers Before Bread." For example, many of the affiliates provide luxurious vacations for elderly persons. The Chicago affiliate maintains two vacation homes: one in Rochelle, Illinois, and one on Lake Delavan, an exclusive resort area in Wisconsin. Combined, the homes provide a week's vacation each year for approximately 370 elderly people. Persons are selected based on the length of time they have been with the project and whether they have ever been able to afford a nice vacation.

The Lake Delavan site accommodates 10 persons for a week's vacation, 13 weeks a year. During the week, the elderly persons have an opportunity to dine in fine restaurants and to take advantage of other entertainment opportunities in the area. For elderly persons, some of whom have known only years of abandonment and neglect, this is a rare opportunity not only to enjoy the simple pleasures that help to make life worth living but—more importantly— to learn to value and appreciate themselves.

Little Brothers has not sought government or United Way funding. It based this decision on the expectation that funds expended for luxury items for elderly persons would appear in an audit as questioned costs. They have relied instead on private donations. They also raise funds through antique auctions—the antiques donated from French supporters.

Henry David Thoreau once said that if he knew someone was coming to his house to help him, he would flee in terror. His terror was perhaps based on the suspicion that anyone coming to help had their own agenda in mind—the helper was coming with an idea as to how Thoreau should lead his life. However, Thoreau might have approved of Little Brothers' approach. Knowing the person was coming in friendship, he might have stayed and looked forward to the visit.

Young persons advocate for institutional change within the community to benefit the frail, homebound elderly.

• The Kansas State University at Manhattan sponsors a project entitled Elderserve. The project seeks to improve the quality of life for elderly persons living in small rural communities using teams composed of three to four upper-level students, men and women, and a faculty mentor. The students are expected to commit at least 100 hours of service during the semester.

In Summerfield, Kansas, the only grocery store was about to close. This was a critical issue facing the entire community, but the frail elderly would suffer the most. As in rural communities across America, the majority of the residents are elderly. The students met with the residents to explore the possibility of establishing a food cooperative. However, because of the interest generated by the students, the owner of the grocery store decided not to close but to stay in the community.

In talking with the residents, the students learned that the community was facing another hardship—the town's only newspaper had gone out of business. With the help of the students, the citizens started their own monthly newsletter, The New Summerfield Sun. The newsletter has now gone through six issues and, although the students have left, the newsletter is continuing, reducing the sense of isolation among elderly persons and, for everyone, helping to maintain a sense of community.

In Dodge City, Kansas, the students helped to create a job skills data bank. The students wanted to implement in a very practical way the concept of "productive aging," where the elderly population is seen not just as needing services but as a population with an immense body of skills, knowledge, and wisdom. They identified, among others, retired teachers, homemakers, plumbers, and carpenters. The students then surveyed potential employers who were seeking people with these skills and were interested in employing them for one or two days a week. The concept of productive aging encourages people to look at elderly persons not only in terms of what they lack but also in terms of what they have to offer. In terms of self-esteem, this approach is very important. Everyone has something to offer.

In Council Grove, Kansas, a different approach was used by another team of students. They surveyed the residents to assess their interest in a senior center. The survey took on a life of its own. As the citizens met and discussed the needs facing their community, they decided that what they needed was a community center—a place where not only elderly persons could meet but also children, young adults, families. The community center had the support of everyone, young and old alike. A meeting was held where more than 200 people turned out—a phenomenon in a small rural community. The mayor and other officials are implementing the plan, and the community expects to have their center within two years.

In analyzing the projects involving the food cooperative and the community center, it is important to note that, after the students initiated the surveys, the dynamics of the situation took over. The students allowed the dynamics to work, without trying to impose their own preconceived ideas about what was best for the elderly people in the community. The students learned about politics and about life. And the needs of elderly persons were addressed—not as something apart from the rest of the community and somehow competing with other elements of the community, but as an integral, legitimate part of the community.

Two examples of multifaceted endeavors based within ethnic groups

As examples of multifaceted endeavors based within ethnic groups, two additional projects should be mentioned: the Pascua Yaqui Tribe Liogue Senior Center and DOROT.

• Tony Sanchez, Executive Director of the Pascua Yaqui Tribe Liogue Senior Center, explained how intergenerational programs operate on Indian reservations. In the tradition of the extended family, the young and elders support each other. The senior center sponsors a baseball team, called the Pascua Pumas. Across the front of the uniforms is emblazoned "Liogue Senior Center." Every year the team sponsors a "Fathers' Day" game and a "Mothers' Day" game as a way of saying thanks.

The young people work in the Tribe's senior center doing various chores: helping to serve the food, writing letters, and acting as liaisons with social service organizations. One young man donated a beautiful painting to the center. The painting depicts the entire history of the Tribe, including the earliest days, through the Spanish conquest, to the present day. Young people also visit the elders in nursing homes.

In the autumn, a day is set aside for the young to remember the elders who have passed away during the year. The favorite dishes of the elders are prepared. Books containing the family trees of the deceased are placed on the table. From a cup, water is sprinkled north, south, east, and west. All those present then drink some water from the cup. A tablecloth is placed on the ground and the food is moved from the table to the earth. Again, all those present partake of the food. In this way, the departed souls of the elders are remembered and comforted in their journey. The young have an opportunity to show their respect for the elderly departed and the community is drawn together—young persons and elderly persons, the living and the departed.

Because of limited housing and because of the extended family tradition within the Indian community, few elderly live alone on the reservation. When younger people help older people, the help is offered either as a member of the family or within the context of the Tribe. For the Pascua Yaqui Tribe, the Liogue Senior Center acts as a focal point for the community. Through the senior center, the young and elderly are able to meet and to help each other.

• "DOROT" means "generations" in Hebrew. The DOROT program in New York brings the generations together. The program was started 14 years ago by a few students from Columbia University who saw the plight of elderly Jews and decided to reach out to them through friendly visiting and holiday package deliveries. With a staff of 34 persons and more than 1,500 volunteers, the program now serves 1,300 elderly persons each year. Compassionate and imaginative, the staff of social workers and administrators attempts to use a variety of methods to reach the homebound.

DOROT has a telephone "university" where, several times each week, elderly persons learn about and discuss issues that affect their lives. They also pursue subjects of personal interest: the Torah, current affairs, music, literature. If a student has a particular interest or skill, he or she may soon be leading a class. Speaker phones are provided to those who need them.

The university not only provides elderly persons with an opportunity to be life-long learners, but it also enhances the self-esteem of the students. One woman said: "I feel better about myself now that I am a university student." The classes are not simply lectures, but lively discussions where personal opinions and feelings are freely shared.

The pleasure and excitement of learning something new continues throughout life. At the end of each term, which lasts three months, the students have an opportunity to meet in person and share a meal together. When you meet your fellow students, are they as you expected them to be? She answered: "No, not at all. I am always surprised, and sometimes disappointed."

Wandering minstrels come to visit the frail elderly homebound. Musicians volunteer time to come to their homes and play. One professional musician brings his recorder to entertain the frail elderly. He says the music not only breaks through the person's sense of isolation and depression but also helps the person to smile and relax. For an hour, pain and loneliness are forgotten. Another dimension is opened up, and the world of beauty and peace is again discovered. But not always. When offered the opportunity to hear the musician, one man declined, saying he did not consider the recorder a musical instrument worthy of attention.

During holidays, special gift packages are prepared for elderly, homebound persons. The packages contain everything from necessities to the whimsical. The delight in opening a gift is not limited to children, but is a joy everyone can appreciate. From all over New York and beyond, volunteers come to pack and deliver these holiday packages. At this time, an informal audit of the elderly persons is done. The volunteer is asked to complete a questionnaire: Did the elderly person appear to be in need of medical attention? Was the person depressed? Was the person living in a healthy environment? Were any special problems noted?

This visit may be one of the few they will receive during the year. For this reason, the observations of the volunteer are important. DOROT notifies the responsible social agencies of situations where elderly persons appear to need help. Also, during this time, new volunteers are recruited. Although DOROT will never be able to reach all the thousands of lonely homebound elderly in New York, each new volunteer means a special friend to someone living alone.

Through their friendly visiting program, DOROT brings a ray of light into a dark room. Even when not physically incapacitated, many elderly persons in New York are fearful of leaving their homes or apartments. Their fear of walking the streets alone further isolates them and severely limits their world. A friendly visitor makes it possible for them not only to go shopping but also to take a walk in the park, feel the sunshine, and hear the sound of laughter. For those in need, friendly visitors also bring a week's supply of kosher food. These visitors are DOROT's "Meals on Heels" volunteers.

DOROT assigns a social worker for a certain number of volunteers. Working with the volunteers, the social worker provides professional guidance and acts as an advocate for the older persons. They not only receive companionship for a couple of hours each week, they also have a social worker who will help them to receive additional benefits, such as food assistance, clothing, or medical care.

DOROT goes beyond serving the homebound elderly and also reaches out to the homeless elderly. Provided rooms in an SRO (single room occupancy) hotel, the homeless elderly are given a place to stay until they are able to find permanent residence. While elderly persons are at the SRO, social workers from DOROT act as advocates and counselors. The social workers determine benefits for which the person may be entitled, assist in completing the necessary forms, and perform the necessary follow-up work.

If relatives are in the area, and if the elderly person grants permission, the relatives are contacted. At the SRO, volunteers come to visit and prepare and serve meals. Persons who are currently abusing drugs or alcohol are not permitted to stay at the SRO, but other sources of help are sought for them. Inclusion of aftercare has been central to the success of the program. After the person has found permanent residence, DOROT continues to follow up to help ensure that the person does not again become homeless.

When DOROT first began 14 years ago with a few dedicated college students, the volunteers operated out of the basement of a synagogue. DOROT now receives funding from several sources and has its own offices; however the relationship with synagogues is still central to DOROT's work. Volunteers are recruited from synagogues for friendly visiting, and synagogues host programs for DOROT's elders. A special relationship is also maintained with Columbia University, a continuing source of student volunteers.

DOROT is a good example of how a strong ethnic community can initiate and maintain volunteer services for elderly, homebound persons. The sense of community creates a place for elderly people and creates a sense of responsibility for the young. The volunteers now come from all age groups—only about a third of the volunteers are high school or college students. However, college students started DOROT and, as the name implies, the impulse for the program came from the students' pride in their religious and ethnic identity and their sense of responsibility to help the older generation.

INDEX TO PROJECT PROFILES

Let Us Serve Them All Their Days • 35

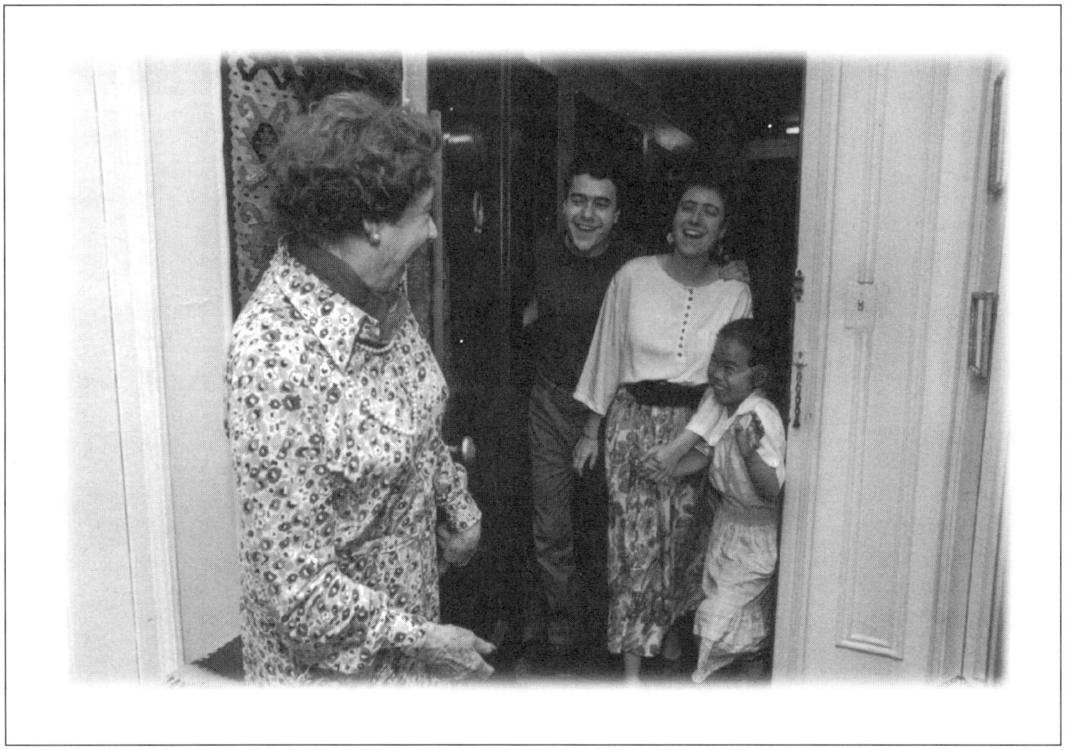

In the following section, we will present the projects under the headings of Help/Maintenance Projects, Meal Delivery Projects, Home Services Projects, Telephone Reassurance Projects, and Other Service Projects. This index is offered as an additional guide to the profiles.

Cross-generational. Includes mentoring-type projects where older people provide emotional support to younger volunteers and act as role models. Also includes tri-generational projects where adults supervise young volunteers performing work for elderly persons.

Indiana — page 87
Michigan — pages 59 and 108
New York — pages 122 and 151

Ohio — page 62
Pennsylvania — page 93
Texas — pages 50 and 51

Residential. Projects where young volunteers share residences with older adults. Also, projects where volunteers receive residential accommodations or reduced rent.

California — page 146
Kansas — page 139

Ohio — page 77
Pennsylvania — page 145

Scholarships/Internships/Stipends/Rewards. Projects where volunteers are eligible for scholarships, internships, stipends, and special rewards based on service.

California — page 85
Kansas — page 104
Louisiana — page 141

New York — pages 115 and 122
Pennsylvania — page 94

Service credit. Projects where the volunteers earn service credits that may be redeemed for service for themselves or transferred to others in need of service.

California — page 147
Louisiana — page 141

Michigan — page 142

Let Us Serve Them All Their Days • 37

Academic credit. Projects where volunteers may receive academic credit.

California — page 98

Indiana — page 101
Iowa — page 132

New York — pages 48, 60, 76, 116, 121, 122, and 150
Texas — page 127
Vermont — page 128

Stay-in-School. These projects are specifically designed to encourage the volunteers to stay in school or, if they have dropped out, to return to school.

Iowa — 55

New York — pages 122 and 143

Skill learning/Employment training/Employment. These projects are structured to provide the young person with work-readiness and vocational skills.

California — page 97
Iowa — pages 54, 55
Louisiana — page 56
Maine — pages 46, 57

Michigan — pages 58, 59
Missouri — page 75
New York — page 151
Pennsylvania — page 94

Volunteers with mental, emotional, or behavioral problems. These projects provide support and guidance to volunteers who experience mental, emotional, or behavioral problems.

Florida — page 73
Indiana — page 87

Iowa — page 148

Specialized volunteer training provided. These projects provide specialized training courses for the volunteers

California — pages 84, 96, and 97
Idaho — page 100
Kansas — page 139
Maryland — page 107
Minnesota — page 90

New York — page 119
North Carolina — page 123
Pennsylvania — pages 91 and 92
Tennessee — page 126

Partnership projects. Projects are jointly sponsored by two or more agencies.

>| | |
>|---|---|
>| California — page 85 | New York — page 143 |
>| Massachusetts — page 88 | Ohio — page 124 |
>| Minnesota — page 89 | Washington, D.C. — page 86 |

Sliding Scale. These projects involve contributions based on income.

>| | |
>|---|---|
>| California — page 99 | Texas — page 127 |
>| New York — page 48 | |

Fund-raising. These projects have succeeded in raising funds using both traditional and innovative approaches.

>| | |
>|---|---|
>| Alabama — page 72 | Kentucky — page 106 |
>| Indiana — page 101 | New Jersey — page 112 |
>| Iowa — page 132 | New York — pages 117, 121, 122, and 143 |
>| Kansas — page 105 | Utah — page 136 |

Let Us Serve Them All Their Days • 39

Project Profiles

· · · · · · · · · · · · · ·

YOUNG PEOPLE SERVING HOMEBOUND ELDERLY PEOPLE

Help/maintenance Projects

Let Us Serve Them All Their Days • 41

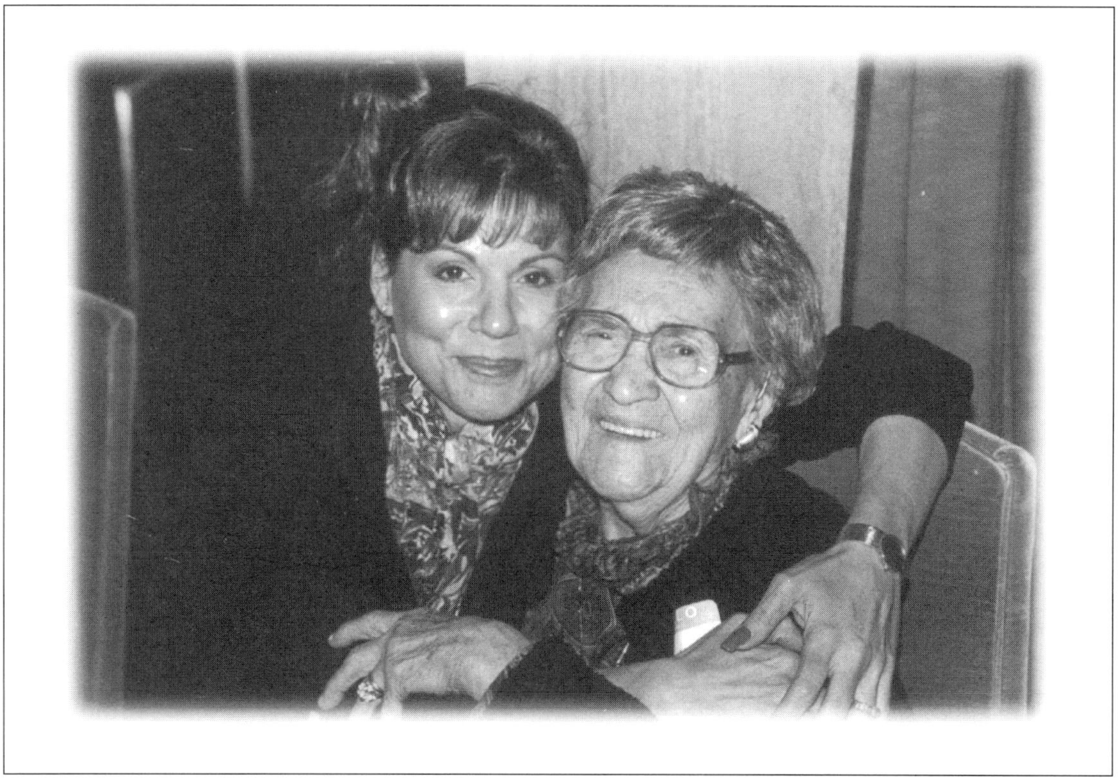

Introduction

Help/maintenance projects frequently make it possible for elderly persons to continue to live safely and independently. A broken step, a missing handrail, the lack of a grip bar—all can spell disaster for an elderly person. As we mentioned earlier, a simple fall often results in hospitalization and, subsequently, loss of independence. Through intergenerational programs, a young person has an opportunity to learn new skills and to use these skills to help another person.

The types of activities are almost limitless. For example, as we describe later in the H.E.A.R.T. project in Jacksonville, Florida, "Entire roofs are replaced, floorboards repaired, windows, doors and screens are replaced, yards cleaned and houses painted inside and out." Or in the Community Services Program in Belmont, Massachusetts, activities include, "...raking leaves, washing windows, cleaning out cellars, planting, pruning, lawn care, cleaning ovens, mopping floors, and moving air-conditioners." In Lufkin, Texas, the United Methodist ARMY activities include, "... building and repairing wheelchair ramps, handrails, porches, windows, roofs, and floors, as well as yard work and painting. "

Frequently not only is the labor donated, but the material—the paint, the brushes, the lumber—are also donated. In some projects, each volunteer gives a fixed amount to cover the costs of the materials, or a special fund-raising event is held to cover the cost.

However, purists beware. We have included projects where young people are paid a small wage. Many projects—designed to keep young people in school, or to encourage them to return to school—know that often these young people simply cannot afford to live without some income. Due to the importance of these projects in helping both younger and older people, we have included a representative sample.

Name of Project/Program:

Lutheran Social Services of Northeast Florida's H.E.A.R.T. Program (Helping Elderly Attain Repairs Today)

• •

Contact Person:

Deborah L. Karably
Grants Coordinator
Lutheran Social Services of Northeast Florida
P. O. Box 41514
421 W. Church Street, Suite 322
Jacksonville, FL 32202

904-632-0022

Project/Program Description:

H.E.A.R.T. provides no-cost home repairs for the low-income elderly. Entire roofs are replaced; floorboards repaired; windows, doors and screens are replaced; yards cleaned; and houses painted inside and out. The latter two services are frequently provided by youth groups recruited through churches and high schools.

A common profile of a H.E.A.R.T. Program recipient is a 75-year-old widow who has resided alone for 10 years and is in frail health. The youth groups bring much more than a clean-up crew to elderly persons. They bring a renewal of faith in the generosity of youth, and in the realization that true "community" still exists in our society.

Another activity is the "Servant Event," held once a year and locally co-sponsored by Lutheran Social Services. Each summer, the Lutheran Church-Missouri Synod sponsors teens nationwide to provide a week of community service. The young people earn their own money to participate in the program, and, in addition to the expenses, each youth donates money toward the purchase of needed materials. For eight hours a day, five days in a row, these "servants" donate their time and talents and share their love with the elderly homeowners.

Name of Project/Program:

Community Service Program Volunteer Services to the Elderly

• •

Contact Person:

Donna David, Community Service Coordinator
Belmont Hill School
350 Prospect Street
Belmont, MA 02178

617-484-4410

Project/Program Description:

In its Community Service Program, Belmont Hill School conducts two major activities dealing with volunteer services to elderly persons.

Two groups of students, upper-school and middle-school, volunteer to be on a "work crew" to help local elderly people who need help with chores, such as raking leaves, washing windows, cleaning out cellars, planting, pruning, lawn care, cleaning ovens, mopping floors, and moving air-conditioners.

Every Friday morning, 7th and 8th grade students leave the school at two separate times for 40 minutes to visit the residents at two separate local elderly housing projects. Besides delivering bread, croissants, rolls, and bagels (which are donated by a local merchant, and picked up by another group of students the day before they are delivered), the young students visit with the elderly residents and do small chores, such as flipping a mattress or moving furniture so the area underneath can be swept (if other help is needed, this is scheduled for another time). The residents from these two housing projects are also invited, for free, to attend matinees at school plays.

These programs are well supervised by the school faculty and staff, and have had great benefits for all involved. Many friends have been made over the years between the younger persons and the older persons.

Name of Project/Program:

Community Service Project (CSP)

• •

Contact Person:

Program Director
Community Service Project
346 Main Street
Rockland, ME 04861

207-594-2221

Project/Program Description:

Volunteers, between the ages of 12 and 16, provide home maintenance services to older residents within a 20-mile radius of Rockland (Knox County). This assistance allows many senior citizens to continue living at home.

Teams of three students and one supervisor perform various services, including basic repairs, yard work, painting, snow shoveling, wheelchair ramp construction, weatherizing, and grocery shopping. A $20 annual Community Service Project membership fee is charged the volunteers.

During the year, training workshops are offered for the volunteer students. After 30 hours of service work and at least one training workshop, the student receives a Community Service Project patch and is eligible for a reward trip. Following 40 hours of service work and two training workshops, the student may participate in an apprenticeship—a non-paid, local work experience in the field of the student's choice. After 50 hours of service and three training workshops, the student is eligible for paid employment.

Supervised students are paid minimum wage for work for non-Community Service Project customers who hire for services. A sliding-scale fee is provided for Community Service Project customers, based on annual income.

The project is governed and evaluated by a board of directors. Support for the project is provided by fees, foundation grants, fund-raising events, and donations.

Name of Project/Program:

Little Brothers, Friends of the Elderly

• •

Contact Person:

Michael Aten
914 Royce Road
Hancock, MI 49930

906-482-6944

Project/Program Description:

The Little Brothers sponsor various projects that assist elderly persons who live alone, on limited incomes, and frequently without support from their families. Activities includes friendly visiting, chore service, and a wood program that provides heating wood for elderly persons living in rural areas.

The project was initiated in May 1982. More than 150 students from the Michigan Technological University of Houghton volunteer for a minimum of eight hours each month. Approximately 80 elderly persons are visited in their homes, with more than 450 persons served in nursing homes. The project is supported by private contributions and by funds from corporations, foundations, and local businesses.

Name of Project/Program:

Home Help for Seniors

• •

Contact Person:

Debra Sponable
Home Help for Seniors Program
The Regional Council on Aging
1945 Five Mile Line Road
Penfield, NY 14526-1048

716-586-8921

Project/Program Description:

Non-medical home support services are provided to older persons to help them live independently at home. Young volunteers, and others, provide the following services: friendly visits; housecleaning and yard work; home repairs and safety checks; meals at home or at a senior center; transportation, errands, shopping; help with bathing or dressing; and respite care.

Sponsored by the Regional Council on Aging, many of these services to elderly persons are either free of charge or on a sliding scale based on ability to pay. Donations are encouraged.

Recruitment of volunteers is through press releases, brochures, and direct contact with groups. Volunteers are asked to make a commitment of 40 weeks. They receive 10 hours of initial training. Academic credit is available. An annual award reception is held, with Christmas cards and gifts for the volunteers.

About 500 seniors are served each year. Two hundred volunteers and twelve staff persons participate. The funding level for Chore Service is $20,000 per year; and for Respite Service, $26,000 per year.

The program is supported by the United Way of Greater Rochester, Monroe County Community Development Administration, the Town of Gates, the Town of Penfield, the Town of Webster, the Fairport-Perinton Senior Living Council, and the Church of the Incarnation.

Name of Project/Program:

People Under Mission to People (PUMP)

• •

Contact Person:

W. Gerald Witt
Connellsville Area Community Ministries
201 East Fairview Avenue
Connellsville, PA 15425

411-626-1120

Project/Program Description:

Young people volunteer to repair homes, clean up property, fix windows, and repair bathrooms for elderly community residents. The program has been in operation for seven years.

Other Connellsville Community Ministries' projects include soup kitchens, a clothing program, and emergency food boxes. These services, which have been provided for the last 14 years, involve more than 350 volunteers.

Volunteers are recruited by advertising in regional offices, through national religious organizations, and the Commission on Religion in Appalachia (CORA). The program is not affiliated with any school. Youth and adult volunteer groups receive certificates of appreciation.

These programs are sponsored by the Connellsville Area Community Ministries (CACM). One staff person coordinates the projects. Each group, both college and church groups, that volunteers must pay its own expenses, and provide funds for its own project.

Name of Project/Program:

Y.E.S. (Youth Exchanging with Seniors)

• •

Contact Person:

Betty Stout, Ph.D.
Associate Professor
Education, Nutrition and Restaurant/Hotel Management
College of Home Economics
Texas Tech University
Lubbock, TX 79409-1162

806-742-3189

Project/Program Description:

The intergenerational, interagency, community-based Y.E.S. project links Future Homemakers of America and 4-H members with senior citizens in a twenty-county region of West Texas to provide assisted-living services for senior citizens. A County Resource Team comprised of an Extension home economist, a home economics teacher, and a health care professional or senior citizen coordinate the project in each county.

This team enlists a variety of community volunteers from business, health care, and civic/service organizations to teach the youth service providers and to match them with senior citizens requesting services. Seniors also work with youth to carry out a joint project that will benefit the community or county.

Suggested assisted-living services for senior citizens that may be offered include: routine housekeeping, lawn care, personal services, minor auto care, and minor home repairs. Y.E.S. volunteers work with their County Resource Team and community volunteer leaders to deliver individual services to elderly persons in the Project's 18,000 square mile region.

Funding sources include: the Robert Wood Johnson Foundation, the West Texas Chamber of Commerce Foundation, the South Plains Foundation, the Texas Department on Aging, and funding from various corporate and private contributions.

Name of Project/Program:

U. M. ARMY (United Methodist Action Reach-Out Mission by Youth, Inc.)

• •

Contact Person:

Susan Hageman, Executive Director
U.M. ARMY
(United Methodist Action Reach-Out Mission by Youth)
P. O. Box 96
Lufkin, TX 75902-0096

409-634-1677

Project/Program Description:

In this ministry, youth and adults provide home repairs for those unable to help themselves. They experience work, fellowship, worship, and fun daily. Participants report that they learn a great deal about themselves and others. Groups travel at least an hour from home and meet with others at a United Methodist church where they spend a week working in the community.

Participating high-school-age youth groups pool their resources of leadership, tools, transportation, and materials. Each participating church sends one adult, who is 21 years or older. The church is asked to pay for the adult's expenses. Most adults work with a team of four or five youths, driving them to work sites in their own vehicles.

Other adults may be a part of the leadership team of the camp, acting as camp director or coordinator of safety, food, sites, tools, programs or administration. The Texas Department of Human Services provides most of the work referrals, though some come from ministers and other agencies.

Common projects include building and repairing wheelchair ramps, handrails, porches, windows, roofs, and floors, as well as yard work, painting, and visitation. Both the youths and the adults pay a fee of $115.

Several of the following help/maintenance projects are smaller in scope and funding than the preceding projects. However, projects come in all sizes and shapes, just as younger people and older people do. And all of the projects have something to teach us and to inspire us.

Name of Project/Program:

Intergenerational Activities in North Central Connecticut

• •

Contact Person:

Cassandra H. Johnson, Executive Director
North Central Connecticut Area Agency on Aging, Inc.
999 Asylum Avenue, Suite 500
Hartford, CT 06105

203-724-6443

Project/Program Description:

Young people volunteer to provide chore and friendly visiting services to frail elderly persons under the sponsorship of the Hockanun Valley Community Council. These services are also provided to elderly persons through the Town of Bolton.

Under the sponsorship of the North Central Connecticut Area Agency on Aging, young people work with the frail elderly at the Hebrew Home and Hospital, the work centering around gardening and horticulture. In addition, the organization also conducts intergenerational activities with frail elderly and students, on a continuing basis, at adult day centers that are co-located with pre-school programs.

Area program is supported under Title III of the Older Americans Act.

Name of Project/Program:

Earlham Service Learning Program

• •

Contact Person:

Connie L. Harris, Director
The Service Learning Program
Earlham College
Box 195-E
Richmond, IN 47374

317-983-1317

Project/Program Description:

Approximately 300 Earlham College students assist older people with transportation, home and yard maintenance, and home repair. Academic credit is available through a college internship in human development and social relations. Elderly persons are referred by the Area Nine Agency on Aging. The college provides most of the funds.

Name of Project/Program:

Operation Threshold

• •

Contact Person:

Patti J. Kuebler, Executive Director
Operation Threshold
300 West Third Street
Waterloo, IA 50701

319-235-6243

Project/Program Description:

Initiated approximately 8 years ago by the City of Cedar Falls, the program has a two-fold purpose: to provide employment for teenage youth, and to perform needed household chores for the low-income elderly and disabled to help them remain in their homes.

The program is funded annually by Community Development Block Grant funds. Activities include lawn-raking and mowing, snow shoveling, cleaning of garages and basements, minor household tasks such as vacuuming, washing dishes, and cleaning kitchens and bathrooms.

Name of Project/Program:

New Horizons Program

• •

Contact Person:

Ronald Sallade, Supervisor
New Horizons Program
1800 Grand Avenue
Des Moines, IA 50309

515-242-7890

Project/Program Description:

Approximately 100 high school age students provide chore services, lawn mowing, and the painting of homes for elderly persons and persons with handicaps. The youths are a part of a dropout prevention/dropout retrieval program which uses closely monitored, paid work experience as part of a strategy in helping students attend school more regularly and complete high school.

Name of Project/Program:

Youth Homemaker Services for the Elderly

• •

Contact Person:

Barbara J. Hill
LaFourche Community Action Agency
P. O. Box 267
Thibodaux, LA 70302

504-446-6731

Project/Program Description:

Under the supervision of the LaFourche Community Action Agency, young people age 16 years and older work six to eight weeks during the summer, receiving minimum wage. They provide homemaker services to the frail, homebound elderly in the community.

Funding for this program is through a Job Training Partnership Act (JTPA) contract with the Work Connection.

Name of Project/Program:

Community Service Project

• •

Contact Person:

Perry Gates
Projects, Inc.
Box 261
Camden, ME 04843

207-594-2636

Project/Program Description:

Teenagers are taught basic skills in home maintenance and repair which they, in turn, apply to the needs of elders with limited incomes. The teenagers are supervised by adult mentors in this intergenerational community service project.

Teams of students visit the homes of elders to perform such services as building wheelchair ramps, weatherizing, painting, and making basic home repairs. Users of the services pay modest fees from $2 to $10 per visit, based on a sliding scale. After 30 hours of service, each teenage volunteer is eligible for a "reward trip" which may involve wilderness or coastal backpacking, canoeing, skiing, or sailing.

Name of Project/Program:

Partithership Program

• •

Contact Person:

Cyndi Kagarise
M-D-S Community Action Agency
P.O. Box 148
Manistique, MI 49854

906-341-2452

Project/Program Description:

Youths, ages 12 through 19, provide home repairs for frail elderly in the Manistique area. In the process, they learn skills from the volunteer elderly who also participate in the program. The goal is to provide adolescents with positive volunteer experiences which will promote self-esteem and thereby limit drug use and teenage pregnancies.

The young volunteers are recruited from social services, school counselors, and the courts. Elderly volunteers are chosen on the basis of skills they have to offer. Safety training is given. The program is overseen by the Community Action Agency, and sponsored by the Neighborhood Builders Alliance and the Michigan Department of Social Services.

Name of Project/Program:

Senior Homemaker Services

• •

Contact Person:

Lois Stockman
Senior Homemaker Services
101 E. Willow
Lansing, MI 48906

517-482-1979

Project/Program Description:

Senior Homemaker Services provides homemaker services to promote the dignity and independence of homebound older persons (age 60 or older). Services include light housekeeping, laundry, grocery shopping, and social support. The program is a part of the Capital Area Community Services (CACS) which serves people in the Lansing Capital Area—Clinton, Eaton, Ingham, and Shiawassee Counties.

Neighborhood Youth Corps, another CACS program, is an employment training program for youth 16-21 years of age. The program focuses on youths in the world of work. When appropriate, Senior Homemaker Services combines interested Youth Corp participants with Senior Aides to form work/training teams that repair and make minor improvements in the homes of the homebound elderly.

Senior Home Service is funded by the Older Americans Act, State of Michigan, and by local funding.

Name of Project/Program:

Y.E.S. (Youth Engaged in Service) Volunteer Program

• •

Contact Person:

Karen Maturski, Director
Amherst Y.E.S. Volunteer Program
4255 Harlem Road
Amherst, NY 14226

716-839-4570

Project/Program Description:

For 15 years Y.E.S. has served the community by recruiting youth and training them in community responsibility. Last year, 292 high school, middle school, and college students participated in the program. They renovate old homes for the poor in the Buffalo area, assist persons with physical and mental disabilities at social events, and help with social events at local nursing homes. Referrals are made to the program by the senior center.

Recruitment is through school and church presentations and personal invitations by present members. Some academic credit is available. No time commitment is required. Social activities and educational workshops are offered periodically to allow members to get to know one another better as well as to enhance skills. Awards for volunteers are given at an annual reception and dance. In addition to the director and the assistant director, the project has one full-time staff member. The project is funded by local government and private donations.

Name of Project/Program:

Aging Handyman Program

• •

Contact Person:

Mary Gardner-Smith
Volunteer Coordinator
Allegheny County Office for the Aging
17 Court Street
Belmont, NY 14813

716-268-9390

Project/Program Description:

Older persons often give up their homes, or live in substandard housing, because they are no longer able to keep up with minor home repairs, and have difficulty finding affordable and reliable help. Volunteers from the Alfred State College of Technology Psi Delta Omega's Community Service donated their labor for a special home repair project. The fraternity also gave funds, earned through a bottle return project, to help purchase supplies.

Also, the Allegany County Office for the Aging has a group of experienced handymen to provide minor home repairs. Last year, 343 of these repairs were made. This year, plans are to serve even more older persons.

Name of Project/Program:

Jackson Area Ministries

• •

Contact Person:

Robert Davis
Jackson Area Ministry
PO Box 603
Jackson, OH 45640

614-286-1320

Project/Program Description:

Jackson Area Ministry is a work camping program in southeast Ohio where volunteers are housed in a church and do work projects for the frail elderly and other needy persons. Work includes construction, repair, painting, and yard work.

Volunteers range from junior high school through college students; adults supervise the volunteers on a one to five ratio. Commitment is for one week. Volunteers are recruited from church youth groups of all denominations.

The program has been in operation for almost 20 years. The local Community Action Agency and the senior centers publicize the program. Elderly persons who are able are asked to contribute to cost of materials. Volunteers pay a registration fee to cover the cost of supplies.

Name of Project/Program:

Work Team

• •

Contact Person:

Cherie Reilly
American Red Cross
P. O. Box 1769
Pittsburgh, PA 15230

412-263-3100

Project/Program Description:

Teams of young people, ages 14 through 18, volunteer to paint the homes of elderly persons and persons with handicaps. The recipients provide the paint and the Red Cross provides brushes, drop cloths, rollers, and trays. The young volunteers work one or two Saturdays per month under the supervision of college student volunteers.

Name of Project/Program:

Baylor University Steppin' Out Program

• •

Contact Person:

Elizabeth D. Palacios, Community Service Coordinator
Baylor University
Department of Student Activities
P.O. Box 97074
Waco, TX 76798-7074

817-755-2371

Project/Program Description:

The Steppin' Out program includes weekly projects by volunteers who work with the homebound elderly and with elderly people in nursing homes. Students visit, clean yards, wash windows, repair equipment, rebuild fences, plant gardens, and run errands.

For community-wide projects, a Steppin' Out Day of Service is held—one in the spring and one in the fall. More than 1,900 students participate in the Spring/Fall Day of Service. Local agencies help identify elderly persons in need of help and may provide funding. Many of the volunteers also contribute funds.

Name of Project/Program:

Elderly and Homebound Outreach Assistance

• •

Contact Person:

Ted Owen
Elderly and Homebound Outreach Assistance
PO BOX 13996
Odessa, TX 79768

915-362-4747

Project/Program Description:

The organization supports a number of intergenerational projects, including:

   a) Teen Toilers: Working with the Church of Christ, teenagers meet on Saturdays during the summertime, divide up into groups, and with donated material, paint the homes of indigent elderly persons, and help clean up their yards;

   b) Emergency Food: Church organizations donate $1500 each year for emergency help to elderly persons. Young volunteers help to deliver the food.

Name of Project/Program:

SERVE (Students Enriching and Responding through Volunteer Efforts)

• •

Contact Person:

Ellen Hill, Coordinator
SERVE/Volunteer Services
Johnson State College
Johnson, VT 05656

802-635-2356 Ext. 257

Project/Program Description:

Students help the frail elderly to maintain their independence by providing the following "wood and windows" services: assisting elderly persons to split and stack wood, rototill gardens, wash windows, and put up storm windows.

SERVE is institutionally funded through Vermont State College. Approximately 150 students, faculty, and staff volunteer each semester.

Name of Project/Program:

Young and Old Stick Together (YOST)

• •

Contact Person:

Fay Alatalo
Elderly Services Unit
Jefferson County Human Services
N3995 Annex Road
Jefferson, WI 53549

414-674-3105

Project/Program Description:

High school students provide services to elderly persons in the Young and Old Stick Together (YOST) program. Participating high schools release students once a week from a study hall for home services to older residents of the community.

Working in teams of two, the students help by mowing lawns, trimming shrubs, putting on or removing storm windows, shoveling snow, doing laundry and house cleaning. Student volunteers receive three hours of training before working in the YOST program.

Name of Project/Program:

ENJOY (East Neighbors Join Old and Young)

• •

Contact Person:

Gloria B. Berman
Near East Side Coalition of Older Adults, Inc.
1400 East Washington Ave.
Washington Square Building   Suite 144
Madison, WI 53703

608-244-5353

Project/Program Description:

In the ENJOY program, East High School students volunteer their time to perform tasks which the area elderly are unable to perform (snow shovelling, spreading mulch, scrubbing floors), as well as friendly visiting and reminiscing.

Commitment of one hour per week by pairs of students. No academic credit is available. Approximately 30 seniors are being helped. Some excellent long-term relationships have been established. Sponsored by the Near East Side Coalition of Older Adults and the Madison School District.

MEAL DELIVERY PROJECTS

Let Us Serve Them All Their Days • 69

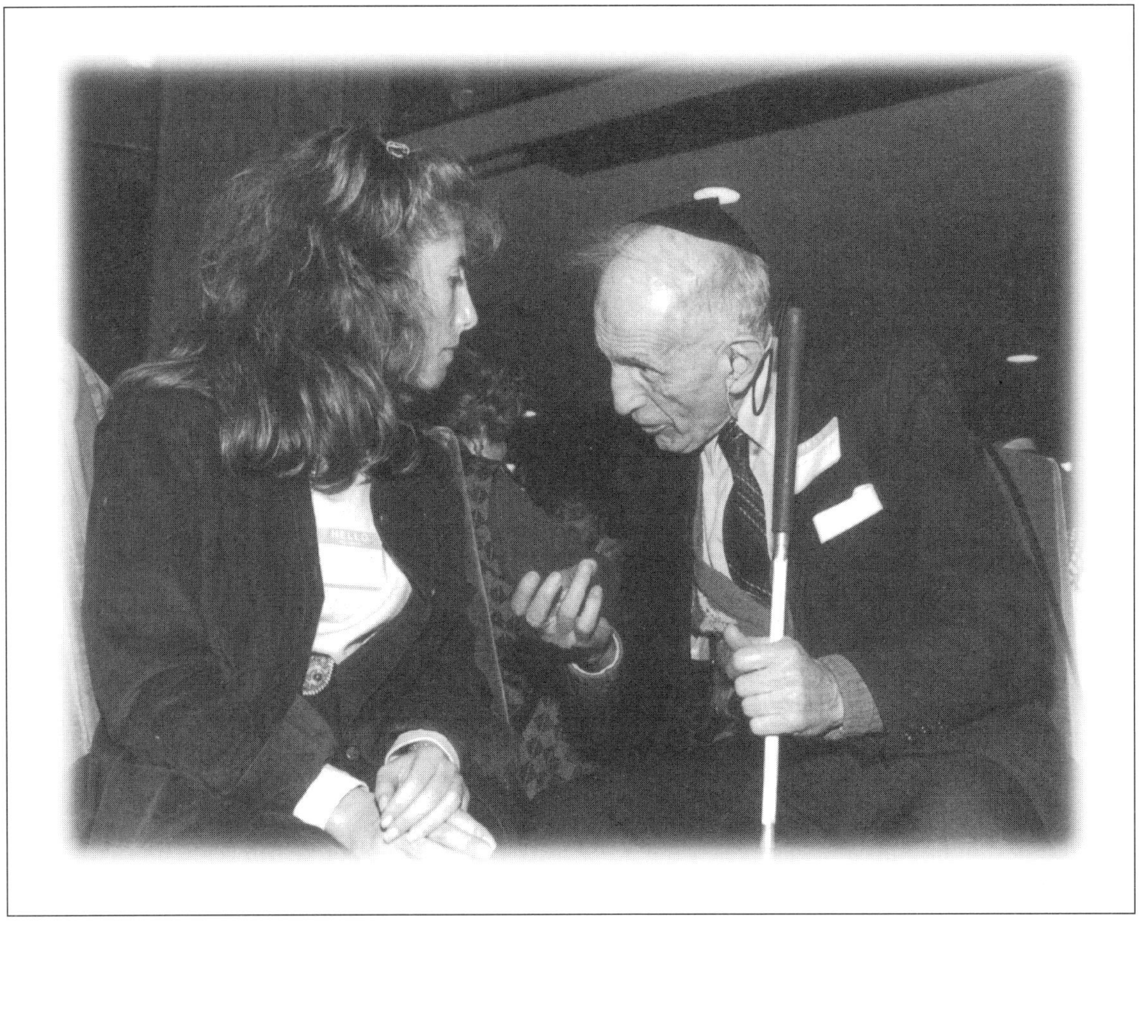

Introduction

Young volunteers often make the difference in whether or not elderly persons will receive a nutritious meal. Traveling across bad country roads in wretched weather during all times of the year, these young people are unsung heroes. And, as in all intergenerational projects, younger and older people discover they have to drop their stereotypes of each other.

The young often see their community in a new perspective. In Texas, one of the young volunteers mentioned that, although he had lived in the area all of his life, he had never realized how much poverty existed and how many people were in need of help. This realization might never have come through simply reading statistics on income distribution.

Name of Project/Program:

Meals on Wheels

• •

Contact Person:

Jane Drewry
Coordinator, Meals on Wheels
or:
Barbara Johnson
Community Service Programs of West Alabama
601 17th St.
Tuscaloosa, AL 35401

205-758-4756 or 205-752-5429

Project/Program Description:

A community program serving a noon meal to the frail elderly. Started as a Title XX program in 1977 for low-income people, in 1981 it became a community program available to all economic groups and financed by the recipients themselves—with churches, clubs, and individuals paying for low-income persons.

Achievements:

Between 40 and 50 young people from the University of Alabama deliver meals during the school semester. The Chancellor Social Club from Stillman College also participates. The program serves 160 people, at $2.10 per meal. Meals are purchased from the Northport Hospital and delivered by volunteers ranging in age from 17 to 83 years. More than 200 volunteers serve 14 routes during the year, with approximately 20 volunteers working each day.

Name of Project/Program:

Neighborly Senior Services' Meals on Wheels Program

• •

Contact Person:

Eleanor L. Reddy, Coordinator of Volunteers
Meals on Wheels
Neighborly Senior Services
13650 Stoneybrook Drive
Clearwater, FL 34622

813-573-9444

Project/Program Description:

Twenty autistic youths, 12 to 20 years old, at Osceola Middle School in Largo help to deliver meals on wheels to Pinellas County homebound elderly. They are assisted by four of their teachers. The autistic youth greatly enjoy this activity, and the elderly persons appreciate their involvement with the program.

American Red Cross Youth, Boy and Girl Scouts, St. Petersburg Junior College, and Eckerd College students also participate in the delivery of meals. The agency's Meals on Wheels Program serves about 1,900 meals a day on 126 routes.

Name of Project/Program:

Project S.E.R.V.E.

• •

Contact Person:

Anita Bohn
Project S.E.R.V.E.
2211 Michigan Union
University of Michigan
Ann Arbor, MI 48109-1349

313-936-2437

Project/Program Description:

Project S.E.R.V.E. provides a variety of volunteer opportunities for University of Michigan students.

Volunteer services to elderly persons include: delivering nutritious meals to the homebound elderly, friendly visiting, and assisting elderly people with tasks and chores necessary for day-to-day existence, thereby helping them to remain independent in their homes as long as possible.

Currently, 50 students volunteer for elderly projects. The funding level for all service projects is $45,000.

Name of Project/Program:

Senior Touch

• •

Contact Person:

Cynthia Kothe
Students Community Services Program
Southeast Missouri State University
805 North Sprigg Street
Cape Girardeau, MO 63701

314-651-2000

Project/Program Description:

Senior Touch pairs low-income older adults with secondary school and university students to help alleviate the isolation of the rural poor who lack private and public transportation. In addition to transportation, other segments of the program include: meal, grocery, and commodity delivery, friendly visiting, reading to the visually impaired, home assessment and repair, and health screening.

The purpose of the program is to enable older adults to become more mobile, to become more aware of and to have greater access to more community services, to consume foods which are more nutritious, and to become more socially and physically active. By gaining first-hand experience working with older adults, students learn the following skills: better communication with older people, identifying loss and life changes, assessment of community services, home safety, nutrition requirements, and how to meet social and emotional needs.

Senior Touch is an intergenerational program operated through Southeast Eldercare Center, Southeast Missouri State University, and funded by ACTION.

Name of Project/Program:

YES (Wyoming Youth Engaged in Service)

• •

Contact Person:

Leslie Tucker, Director
Wyoming County Youth Engaged in Service
26 Linwood Avenue
Warsaw, NY 14569

716-786-8833

Project/Program Description:

Approximately 50 young people volunteer through the Youth Engaged in Service (YES) program and help the homebound elderly through snow shoveling, leaf raking, and delivering hot meals. Volunteers are recruited through classroom presentations and through the schools' Student Government Associations. No stipends, but academic credit may be given.

Volunteers are honored at annual award ceremony. The program is supported by the New York State Division for Youth and the Wyoming County Youth Bureau.

Name of Project/Program:

Oberlin College Community Outreach Office

• •

Contact Person:

Daniel Gardner, Community Outreach Coordinator
Oberlin College
Wilder Hall 221
135 West Lorain Street
Oberlin, OH 44074-1081

216-775-8103

Project/Program Description:

The Community Outreach Office functions as a link between students and agency programs in the area, many of which center on issues affecting elderly persons. Working out of a local hospital, 10 to 15 students deliver hot meals to homebound seniors.

Other projects include: Senior Achievement Center: volunteers help with crafts, outings, games, reading to seniors, and other activities; Oberlin Seniors: volunteers help seniors on insurance and housing problems; and the Jeanne Beattie Butts Intergenerational House: a shared living residence for seniors and residents desiring a family environment, with each age group enriching the lives of the other.

Name of Project/Program:

Metropolitan Inter-Faith Association

• •

Contact Person:

Margaret Fleming
Metropolitan Inter-Faith Association
910 Vance
Memphis, TN 38126

901-527-0208

Project/Program Description:

Under the auspices of the Metropolitan Inter-Faith Association, Memphis has had a home-delivered meals program for elderly persons during the past 16 years. High school youths, Boy Scouts, and college students volunteer.

Many of the high school volunteers receive academic credit for their work. Volunteers are recruited through schools and media. More than 1500 meals are delivered each day. Elderly persons are not charged but donations are accepted. Sponsorship is primarily from private donations, with some federal and local government support.

Name of Project/Program:

United Austin for the Elderly

• •

Contact Person:

Javier L. Garza
United Austin for the Elderly
P. O. Box 6248
Austin, TX 78762

512-474-6416

Project/Program Description:

Using both younger and older volunteers, United Austin administers four projects:

- Meals on Wheels: in 1991, they served 830 recipients over 22,000 meals each month;

- Care Calls: a telephone program that brings friendship and reassurance to elderly people who live alone;

- "Daily Callers" call every morning to check on the elderly person's well-being; "Phone Friends" call two or three times weekly for 30-minute phone visits; and

- Medi-Wheels: a program where volunteers drive elderly people to medical appointments.

HOME SERVICE PROJECTS

Let Us Serve Them All Their Days • 81

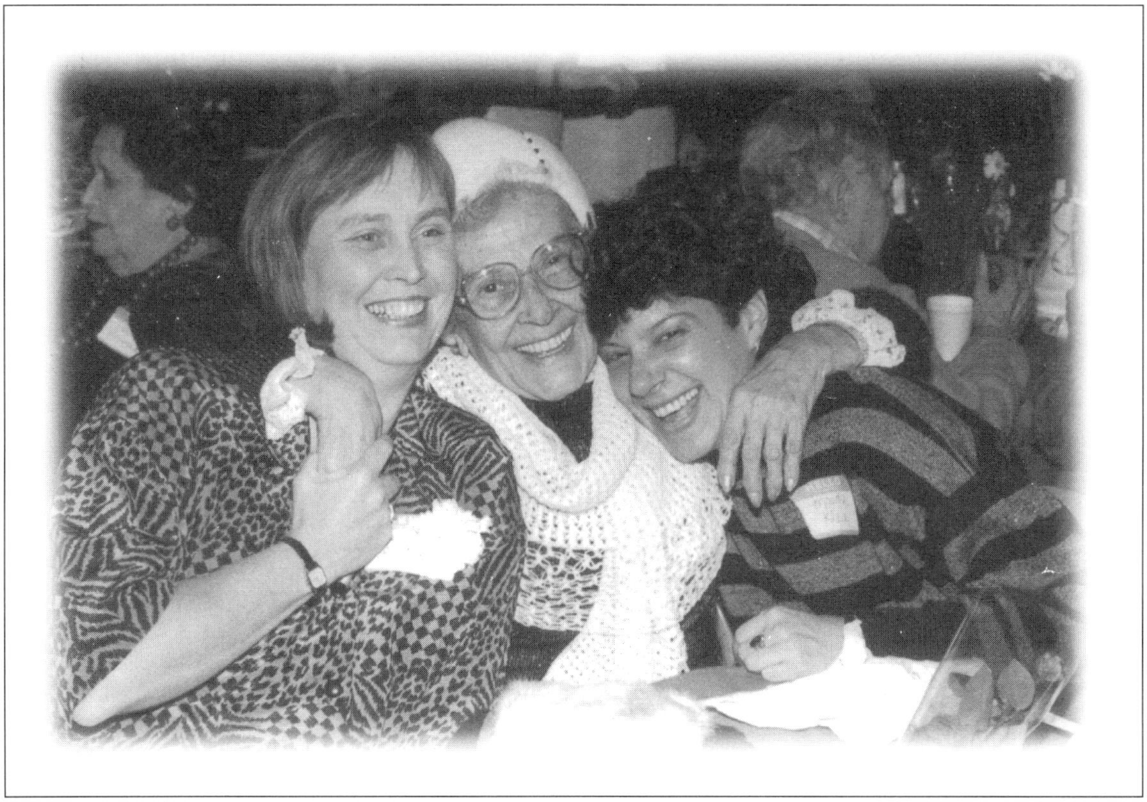

Introduction

"I'll make it, with a little help from my friends." This is an old saying, and true. Many elderly people are able to maintain their independence, provided they are offered some assistance. With a little help from their friends, or friendly volunteers, they are able to stay in their own homes and neighborhoods.

As with the Help/maintenance projects, the types of projects are as limitless as the imagination and as inexhaustible as the energy of youth. In Pittsburgh, Pennsylvania, under the sponsorship of Generations Together, activities include neighborhood walks, outings, shopping, letter reading and writing, reminiscing, board and card games, shared hobbies, and discussion of personal and social issues. In Minneapolis, Minnesota, under the aegis of the Little Brothers—Friends of the Elderly, volunteers provide one-on-one services, such as driving, grocery shopping, preparing meals, running errands, answering the telephone, companionship, sharing interests, social outings, and attending educational in-services on aging-related topics.

Lending a helping hand is a part of our tradition. On the frontier, Americans learned to be rugged individualists. They also learned the value of communal projects, such as barn-raising and quilting. Each member of the family has something important to contribute, and the family learned the importance of caring for each other. Within this tradition of maintaining our independence, living in our own place yet at the same time being a member of the larger community, both as a giver and receiver, "friendly visiting" is as American as the Fourth of July.

Elizabeth Riddleberg has lived in her house for 50 years. She moved back to Koetzletown, Missouri, after her husband died in an accident. She managed to buy a small house with some property for $800. She had three daughters and a son, the youngest was only two years old. 1942. The Depression. With little more than her Social Security check, she reared her four children. Now she is 88 years old, and has no intention of moving. When people talk to her about going to an assisted-living residence, she shakes her head, leans forward on her cane, and says, "No, it just wouldn't be home." Her tone leaves no room for argument. Fortunately for Mrs. Riddleberg, she has family and friends nearby. Once a week, volunteers give her rides to Jefferson City for shopping and for medical appointments. Her family, friends, and volunteers receive their reward. Mrs. Riddleberg is famous for her delicious, homemade bread.

All across the United States, elderly people are desperately trying to maintain their independence. Through a network of family, friends, and volunteers, many are succeeding. We have described some projects that may give you ideas for initiating or expanding your own intergenerational project. We wish you success. Elderly persons, such as Mrs. Riddleberg, need your help.

Name of Project/Program:

Independent Aging Program (IAP)

• •

Contact Person:

Susan S. Alberto
Intergenerational Project Coordinator
Independent Aging Program
2625 Zanker Road
San Jose, CA 95134-3107

408-994-0595

Project/Program Description:

High school and college student volunteers are matched one-to-one with older persons for an intergenerational sharing experience and for service delivery. A student visits an elderly person for two to three hours a week for one year. They do grocery shopping, housekeeping, yard work, friendly visiting, and errands.

Training includes orientation on the Independent Aging Program, case management, and the process of aging. In addition, the volunteers are given in-service training and specialized training on specific disabilities. Quarterly evaluations and monitoring are provided by adult volunteers. A recognition party is held at the end of the school year. Volunteers are recruited through newspapers and assemblies. Students and clients complete evaluation forms at end of the year.

Seventy-two students were actively involved in the program for the 1991-92 school year. Since the program began, more than 1,120 matches have been made. The program is sponsored by Catholic Charities. J. C. Penney has presented awards. Funded by United Way of Santa Clara County, Catholic Charities, individual donors, and corporate and foundation grants.

Name of Project/Program:

Helping Hands

• •

Contact Person:

Angela Wong
Helping Hands Coordinator
Spectrum Community Services, Inc.
1435 Grove Way
Hayward, CA 94546

510-881-0300

Project/Program Description:

The project hires and trains high school students from Hayward and Castro Valley to assist homebound frail elders who are living on a limited income. Students are given a stipend of $4.25 an hour (maximum six hours a week) to help with light housework, grocery shopping, dishes, errands, pet care, light cooking, yard work and gardening, windows, laundry, and friendly visiting. Students attend 12 hours of training, receive individual ongoing support, and attend monthly support group meetings.

In 1992, 65 students were matched with 75 elders. Through the relationships that developed from these matches, the program supports the continued independence of older adults by enhancing their functioning in the community and preventing unnecessary institutionalization. Helping Hands is designed to increase opportunities for youth to gain work experience, earn income, build self-esteem, and develop relationship skills.

The project is sponsored by Spectrum Community Services and Eden Hospital Medical Center, in cooperation with Hayward and Castro Valley Unified School Districts.

Funds are received from the United Way, the City of Hayward, the Morris Stulsaft Foundation, and the community. Volunteers are recruited through press releases and through community outreach and presentations.

Name of Project/Program:

Iona Senior Services

• •

Contact Person:

Kirsten Klingelhofer
IONA Intergenerational Coordinator
IONA Senior Services
4200 Butterworth Place, NW
Washington, DC 20016

202-966-1055

Project/Program Description:

A nonprofit community organization in northwest Washington, D. C., IONA House offers personalized and professional care to people 60 years of age and older. The organization helps frail and active older persons maintain independence and community involvement. IONA House is an alliance of 29 churches and synagogues, community-wide advisory committees, professional staff, and 500 volunteers of all ages.

Most of the volunteers for the intergenerational program come from high schools in the Washington, D.C. area. Currently, approximately 50 young people are involved in the program on a regular basis, although the number of young people and older people served varies throughout the year. Students receive no academic credit for their work, but they may use the hours accumulated through volunteer service toward completing their community service requirement for school. However, many of the students involved in the Friendly Visiting Program volunteer out of sheer desire to help elderly persons and have no community service hours to complete.

A popular project in the Intergenerational Program is Friendly Visiting. Landon School students visit seniors on a regular basis, usually twice a month, and assist with grocery shopping, minor household chores, and yard work. This project gives the young person direct contact with the seniors, perhaps the best experience the student can get in community service work.

Another popular project is Fall & Spring Clean-up. Small groups of students, supervised by adults, help "weatherize" homes. In addition, they rake leaves, mow lawns, dust and vacuum, and perform other household chores necessary to prepare for winter or spring. Several students also volunteer at the IONA Day Health Center, a full-day health, social, and recreational program for mentally and physically frail seniors.

Currently, the annual funding level is $5,000, received through foundation grants.

Name of Project/Program:

Carry-Out Caravan

• •

Contact Person:

Carla J. Gosney
Director, Retired Senior Volunteer Program
1125 Hampshire
Quincy, IN 62301

217-224-3833

Project/Program Description:

Carry-Out Caravan is a grocery-shopping assistance service for frail, elderly persons; persons with handicaps; and homebound persons. Begun in 1983, the program offers a greatly needed service, since the grocery stores in the area do not provide home delivery. Many older and persons and persons with handicaps are unable to shop for themselves or must rely on public transportation, which may be extremely difficult with groceries to carry.

Approximately 30 volunteers from the Adams County Retired Senior Volunteer Program participate in the service by taking and filling the orders and then delivering the orders with groups of boys from the Chaddock School. The school, a residential treatment facility for youth, plays a major role in the project. These young men come from troubled backgrounds and have had few, if any, successes in their lives.

This service learning project teaches the boys that when they help someone else, they increase their own feelings of self-worth and develop better feelings about themselves as individuals. They also learn about the needs and lives of another generation and develop a better understanding of the aging process as they witness the needs of the frail elderly they serve, and the energy of the active elderly that participate as volunteers.

The young men improve the quality of life of the older recipients not only through the service they provide, but also by giving the older persons an opportunity to experience the caring attitude of the younger persons.

Name of Project/Program:

Young at Heart

• •

Contact Person:

Sarah Morgan Taylor
Community Service Center
Boston University
730 Commonwealth Avenue, Room 253
Boston, MA 02215

617-353-4710

Project/Program Description:

Students are paired with older persons on a one-to-one basis. Since 1989, this program has been sponsored by the Community Service Center at Boston University, which addresses the benefits and problems of growing old in America. The relationships between the young people and the older people involve companionship, being a helper, and doing errands for homebound individuals.

Young At Heart volunteers have the choice of working with one or more of four agencies in the Boston area. Boston Aging Concerns and Boston Senior Home Care offer one-on-one match-up programs for volunteers interested in visiting an older person in the Boston area.

The Veronica B. Smith Multi-Service Senior Center offers volunteers the opportunity for drop-in visiting in a group setting. Also, Little Brothers—Friends of the Elderly offers one-time special activities for the holidays.

Time commitments vary with the agency, but most are about two hours per week. Volunteers can request the town and type of person they would like to visit. Training is available and encouraged.

Name of Project/Program:

Acting in the Community Together (A.C.T.)

• •

Contact Person:

Sarah Conning
A.C.T. Coordinator
The A.C.T. Office
One North College Street
Northfield, MN 55057-4010

507-663-4028

Project/Program Description:

A.C.T., in existence since 1985, is a service-based community organization at Carleton College, whose volunteer programs are administered in partnership with local agencies, including the Community Action Center, the senior center, the hospital, a nursing home, and a retirement center.

The Keep-in-Touch program, administered by the Northfield Community Action Center, is another friendly visiting program; volunteers visit homebound elderly residents of Northfield. Another ongoing program is the "Convo Companions" program, in which students accompany seniors from the Northfield Senior Center to the weekly Convocation lecture at Carleton College. The volunteers take their guests to lunch at the college dining hall following the lecture.

In addition to these regular weekly volunteer programs, A.C.T. sends volunteers to work in the Community Action Center's chore service for elderly homeowners in town (such as leaf raking, gardening, and snow removal). The Adopt-a-Grandparent program matches students with residents at a nearby nursing home.

Of about 500 student volunteers sent into the community each year, approximately 50 to 75 students participate in the programs in which they visit and help elderly persons.

Volunteers are recruited through campus publicity and some classes. Orientation varies with type of volunteer activity. No fees are charged or stipends provided. Evaluation is through constant feedback and periodic group sessions. The project has one full-time staff person. A.C.T. is funded by Carleton College and has limited grant funds.

Name of Project/Program:

Little Brothers—Friends of the Elderly

• •

Contact Person:

Liz Lathrop
Little Brothers—Friends of the Elderly
1845 East Lake Street
Minneapolis, MN 55407

612-721-6215

Project/Program Description:

Approximately 2,000 volunteers visit elderly persons to relieve loneliness and isolation. Volunteers include students and adults.

The volunteers provide one-on-one services, such as driving, grocery shopping, preparing meals, running errands, answering the telephone, companionship, sharing interests and social outings, and attending educational in-services on aging-related topics.

Youth volunteer services include: visiting an elderly person in his or her home, apartment, or nursing home two times a month (one-year commitment required); delivering food packages and visiting with elderly who are alone during the holiday season and not attending Little Brothers' holiday dinner (two to three hours commitment on holidays); and teenagers and college students doing painting, minor home repair, yard work, house cleaning, packing and moving for elderly on an on-call basis.

No fees are charged for these services. The program is supported by donations.

Name of Project/Program:

Homefriends

• •

Contact Person:

Adam Brunner, Project Director
Homefriends
Center for Intergenerational Learning
Temple University
1601 North Broad Street, Room 206
Philadelphia, PA 19122

215-787-3196

Project/Program Description:

Approximately 70 students from six local high schools volunteer, in teams of two, to serve 35 homebound elderly. Students provide a variety of chore services, including light housekeeping, laundering, grocery shopping, gardening, and reading bills and other correspondence. The project has been in existence for six years.

Homefriends began as a friendly visiting program, but last year the emphasis shifted toward chore services. The project has experienced success in allowing "friendly visiting" to emerge spontaneously from the chore services. Each school has a coordinator, often a teacher but sometimes a student. Homefriends has reported good success with students acting as coordinators.

Once every three weeks the Project Coordinator from Temple University meets with the volunteers at the various schools to monitor and provide in-service training. New volunteers are given two to four hours of initial training. Students are recruited at assemblies and from student groups, such as the Student Council and the Honor Society. The project is supported from funding from the Montgomery County Aging and Adult Services and from the Public Welfare Foundation.

Name of Project/Program:

Youth In Service To Elders (YISTE)

• •

Contact Person:

James M. McCrea, Program Coordinator
Generations Together
121 University Place, Suite 300
Pittsburgh, PA 15260

412-648-7151

Project/Program Description:

Youth in Service to Elders has for the last nine years served the community's frail elderly by providing weekly scheduled visits between youth and homebound or institutionalized older adults. Since 1982, 200 to 250 young people annually participate in a semester of "friendly visiting" with an equal or greater number of older adults.

Activities include neighborhood walks, outings, shopping, letter reading and writing, reminiscing, board and card games, shared hobbies, and discussion of personal and social issues. Most of the elderly persons participate because they or someone else has expressed a desire for more social contact, especially with young persons. Most of the elderly persons are frail and socially isolated.

The volunteers, age 11 through 22, are recruited from Pittsburgh area schools and service organizations. They commit two hours per week for three months. The volunteers keep time records, attend training, and attend "debriefing" sessions. Those providing 24 hours of service are invited to an annual recognition dinner and receive a certificate of achievement.

Name of Project/Program:

JuniorPARTNERS

• •

Contact Person:

Mrs. Heidi Russman
Senior Partners of Mt. Lebanon
200 Lebanon Avenue
Mt. Lebanon, PA 15228

412-343-3412

Project/Program Description:

Junior and senior high school students were recruited to establish an individual relationship with a senior resident of their community. An initial social event was held to introduce seniors and juniors to each other as a group, and introduction games turned out to be fun for all. One three-hour training session was conducted to teach the students communication skills, how to relate with an older person, and what to do in an emergency.

A part-time staff person was engaged to make matches. More than 30 juniors volunteered in the first recruitment effort. The recruitment of the older persons was not so easy. In some cases, they expressed fears about having a "stranger" in the house, or it seemed like too much trouble. In other cases, it was a fear of making a regular commitment.

A great deal of patience and individual interviews were necessary before matches were made. Referrals came from friends, neighbors, local officials, staff, and board members and were followed up with personal interviews.

As of October 1992, eighteen months after the start of the program, 36 matches had been made. Although many of the older participants are not homebound, a number of them are. The chief criteria for both the younger and older person is a sincere interest in getting to know someone from another generation.

The volunteers range in age from 13 to 18, and the older persons from their late 60s to a 99-year-old legally blind woman living alone. Financial circumstances vary widely.

During their weekly visits, the teens may read to the elderly person, play games, rewrite address books, change light bulbs, or just swap stories about what has been happening since the last week. The matches are closely monitored, and a mid-year evaluation is conducted.

The program is funded by the Trust Department of the Pittsburgh National Bank.

Name of Project/Program:

Youth Engaged in Service

• •

Contact Person:

Francine Gasper Leggett
Volunteer Coordinator
Youth Engaged in Service
Seton Center, Inc.
443 Mt. Thor Road
Greensburg, PA 15601

412-837-1264

Project/Program Description:

Initiated by Seton Center, Inc., in 1984, a Friendly Visitor Volunteer Program seeks to provide a network of volunteers to visit homebound persons on a weekly basis. The volunteers seek to reduce the sense of isolation, to comfort the older persons, to identify any special problems they may have with which the agency can help, to act as linkages within the community, to serve as interpreters of service, to advocate for the inarticulate, and to comfort the homebound elderly by caring and sharing where there is no family or the family has abandoned them. Volunteers range in age from 25 to 85 years. A recognition banquet, with awards and gifts, is held each year.

Youth Engaged in Service is a new endeavor by Seton Center's outreach program to encourage young people, age 16 through 19, to get involved with elderly people, to reach out to the homebound in an attempt to keep them connected with the community and to reduce their sense of isolation, and to identify problems that call for agency intervention. The program also prepares students for the world of work through a supervised work training experience. Through shared experience the program increases the understanding between young people and older adults, and thereby reduces their fears and prejudices about one another.

The teen volunteers visit the older persons at least one hour per week, and perform such activities as reading to the visually impaired; writing letters; helping with meal preparation; gardening; helping frail elderly to health care appointments, bank, or hairdresser; friendly visiting; and making telephone reassurance calls to the homebound.

A $500 scholarship is awarded to the Teen Volunteer of the Year. This is a Seton Center outreach program, sub-contracted by the Westmoreland County Area Agency on Aging.

Several of the following may be more limited in scope and funding that the preceding projects.

Name of Project/Program:

Caring Callers

• •

Contact Person:

Joyce Ellen Lippman, Executive Director
Central Coast Commission for Senior Citizens
Area Agency on Aging
122-C West El Camino
Santa Maria, CA 93454-3610

805-925-9554

Project/Program Description:

More than 100 volunteers, both young and old, participate in an in-home visiting human service project. The purpose of the project is to stimulate, expand, and enhance the social activities of San Luis Obispo County residents who are over 60 years of age, lonely and isolated because of increasing fragile health; separation from family by distance or family indifference; or the death, or moving away, of peers, friends, and neighbors.

The volunteers, who live in the same geographical area, make visits of one hour or more on a weekly basis. Funding level for fiscal year 1991-92 was $41,800. The sources of funding include: Older Americans Act, administered by the local area agency on aging; the United Way of the Central Coast; the County of San Luis Obispo; local cities; and general fund-raising.

Name of Project/Program:

Youth Elderly Services (YES)

• •

Contact Person:

Andrus Gerontology Center
University of Southern California
University Park, MC0191
Los Angeles, CA 90089-0191

213-740-6060

Project/Program Description:

High school students are trained in a broad range of topics related to aging. They are matched with elderly persons, providing them with friendly visiting and other services. Students continue to receive two hours of in-service training each week after they have been matched.

A comprehensive Curriculum Guide and a Facilitator Manual, a total of 320 pages, are available for replicating the YES project developed by the Andrus Gerontology Center at the University of Southern California.

Name of Project/Program:

Resident's Assistance Program (R.A.P.)

• •

Contact Person:

Dr. James Kelly, Director
Department of Social Work
California State University, Long Beach
1250 Bellflower Blvd
Long Beach, CA 90840-0902

310-985-5794

or:

Dr. Susan Rice, Associate Professor
Department of Social Work
California State University, Long Beach
(same address)

310-985-4204

Project/Program Description:

College students visit elderly individuals in their own home, and facilitate support and discussion groups on a weekly basis. This intergenerational individual and group work program also includes two educational workshops and two social potluck dinners each academic year.

These activities take place in Leisure World, a 9,000-member retirement community located adjacent to California State University, Long Beach. Students receive training and supervision as part of their class studies, and then apply that training with the retired persons at Leisure World. Specific problems addressed have to do with widowhood, physical limitations, caring for spouses with Alzheimer's disease, isolation, loneliness, and concerns associated with growing older.

Name of Project/Program:

Human Corps

• •

Contact Person:

Sally Cardenas, Coordinator
Cooperative Education and Volunteer Services
Career Development Center, SS/AD 250
California State University, Long Beach
1250 Bellflower Blvd.
Long Beach, CA 90840-0113

310-985-5553

Project/Program Description:

Students at California State University participate in volunteer community services activities, including services to elderly persons. Services include friendly visiting. Sponsored by the Cooperative Education and Volunteer Services Program of the Career Development Center at California State University, Long Beach. Students may receive elective academic credit through related courses if the volunteer placement meets necessary university requirements.

Name of Project/Program:

OASIS (Older Adult Social Services)

• •

Contact Person:

Yolanda Vasquez, Program Assistant
Fresno-Madera Area Agency on Aging
2220 Tulare Street, Suite 1200
Fresno, CA 93721

209-488-3821

Project/Program Description:

With assistance from student interns of World Impact, Inc., the project offers adult day care in Fresno and Reedley (socialization, stimulation, supervision of dependent elderly), full weekend care at the OASIS house (for dependent elderly, providing time off for caregivers), home care services (meal preparation, housekeeping, shopping assistance, in-home respite), visiting, telephone reassurance, and chore assistance to isolated seniors. Funded by the Fresno-Madera Area Agency on Aging, the City and County of Fresno, and the United Way of Fresno County.

Recommended contributions for services are based on an income-based sliding scale. The programs help elderly persons avoid premature institutionalization.

The number of volunteers varies throughout the year: adult day care and weekend care—25 (all ages); home care/visiting/telephoning/chores—10 (all ages). In addition, seniors receive visits from a nearby preschool.

Name of Project/Program:

How to Help Grandma and Grandpa

• •

Contact Person:

Doris K. Williams, Research and Extension Specialist
Human Development and Gerontology
School of Home Economics
University of Idaho
Moscow, ID 83843

208-885-7234

Project/Program Description:

A 4-H intergenerational program consisting of a one-session course to help young people understand the needs of elderly people and develop a sensitivity to their feelings. Afterwards, the young people are matched with older people for friendly visiting and other services. Seven to ten volunteers are involved. In addition, "Faculty Development in Intergenerational Programming," a one-day meeting, provides programming resources for state Extension staff.

Name of Project/Program:

Serving the Homebound

• •

Contact Person:

Karen Darish, Area 10 Agency on Aging
2129 Yost Avenue
Bloomington, IN 47403

812-334-3383

Project/Program Description:

Ten to fifteen Indiana University volunteers make home visits, provide escort and other services, and assist in the completion of forms. Some volunteers receive academic credit. Minimum commitment is for three hours a week for one semester. The program has been in existence since 1975. Recruitment is through the volunteer fair at Indiana University and various community and student volunteer bureaus. Volunteers are recognized through community award nominations.

The project serves 350 to 400 homebound elderly. During the term of volunteer service, many close friendships develop between the young people and elderly people. The Area Agency on Aging (AAA) evaluates the project and informs elderly people of the project. Funding is obtained from the county, the United Way, the City Community Development Block Grant, and general fund raising.

Name of Project/Program:

Bureau of Refugee Services

• •

Contact Person:

Wayne Johnson
Bureau of Refugee Services
1200 University, Suite D
Des Moines, IA 50314

515-283-7904

Project/Program Description:

Under the direction of the Bureau of Refugee Services, Boy and Girl Scouts of central Iowa work with Southeast Asian elderly refugees. The volunteers range in age from 10 to 13. Approximately 60 volunteers work with 100 elderly persons. The volunteers help with housekeeping, shopping, and gardening.

The goals of the program are to increase the ability of Asian elderly people to function with the community and to give the Boy and Girl Scouts an opportunity to learn about elderly persons and to work with them. The project is supported by small federal grants and by community resources.

Name of Project/Program:

Senior Neighbor Program of Douglas County Senior Services

• •

Contact Person:

Margaret Hopkins
Douglas County Senior Services, Inc.
745 Vermont
Lawrence, KS 66044

913-842-0543

Project/Program Description:

As part of the Senior Neighbor Program, young volunteers—with volunteers of all ages—visit elderly persons on a regular basis and establish friendships. In addition, they provide information about community services and public benefits.

Approximately 150 volunteers and 180 elderly persons participate in the program each year. The volunteers receive training in issues affecting older persons. Funding is through Jayhawk Area Agency on Aging, which provides approximately $5,000 per year for the coordinator's time.

Many schools, church groups, and some university students work with the local Social and Rehabilitation Services Office and Douglas County Senior Services on chore services, providing yard clean-up, and some inside cleaning. These are not regular projects, but are community events on a one-time basis.

Name of Project/Program:

SOAR Volunteer Program for Students

• •

Contact Person:

Cindy Baldwin
SOAR Volunteer Program for Students
Bethany College
421 N. First
Lindsberg, KS 67456

913-227-3891

Project/Program Description:

Student Outreach through Active Response (SOAR) is a volunteer service program at Bethany College, in its fifth year of operation.

One hundred and forty students participate in the volunteer program at Bethany Nursing Home, helping with transportation, crafts, games, and exercise programs, and serving as companions and doing chores for the homebound elderly.

Some academic credit is given, as well as many recognition activities—such as pins, May dinner, and T-shirts. The Community Service Grant Program provides scholarships in return for community service. Current funding level for the entire program is less than $10,000. The program is funded by Bethany College.

Name of Project/Program:

Student Volunteer Service

• •

Contact Person:

Jan Lewis
Johnson County Human Resources and Aging Department
Area Agency on Aging
301A S. Clairborne
Olathe, KS 66062

913-782-7188

Project/Program Description:

Secondary and college age students are recruited and trained as volunteers for the Johnson County Area Agency on Aging. Students serve as companion visitors to low-income homebound seniors. As companion visitors, students offer stimulation and companionship, engaging elderly persons in discussing their life stories and talking about current events. Volunteers are trained to recognize any adverse changes in senior participants and alert agency professionals.

Students also have the opportunity to work on the area agency's current fund-raiser, Savings for Seniors Coupon Program. Students can actively participate in raising funds for the in-home services by working on the coupon program.

Students also have participated in lawn clean-up. Some students assist with meal services and handle telephone emergencies, as well as making birthday and holiday cards for the elderly population in Johnson County.

Name of Project/Program:

Title III/Homecare/Adult Day/Senior Companion/Title V

• •

Contact Person:

Steve Stivers, Director of Aging
Blue Grass Community Action Agency
3445A Versailles Road
Frankfort, KY 40601

502-695-4290

Project/Program Description:

The volunteers range in age from 18 to 87 years old. More than 300 younger and older volunteers are involved, offering friendly visiting in most cases. Commitments are for a year. Volunteers are recruited through various social clubs and by word of mouth. Volunteers receive on-the-job training.

An estimated 3,500 seniors are served by the various programs. The programs serve the Lexington District and nine counties. The programs are staffed with Title III directors, homecare case managers, adult day directors or Senior Companion director, and a Title V director. Financial support is received from various funding agencies, including federal, state, and local government, and the United Way.

Name of Project/Program:

Hands Of Shared Time (HOST)

• •

Contact Person:

Marian Waagbo, Coordinator
Hands Of Shared Time (HOST)
Volunteer Department
Montgomery General Hospital
18101 Prince Philip Drive
Olney, MD 20832

301-774-8629

Project/Program Description:

Young volunteers help elderly with light housekeeping and provide companionship. HOST recruits and trains volunteers from schools, youth groups, civic organizations, and religious congregations. A one-year commitment is required.

A 10-hour training program is provided. Academic credit is given at one local high school. Recruitment is through classroom presentations, lunch-hour sign-ups, and word of mouth in high schools. No fees are charged. The project has received funds from the Kellogg Foundation and from private donations.

Name of Project/Program:

Senior Smiles

• •

Contact Person:

Sheryl Schrot, 4-H Youth Agent
or
Eunice Svinicki, E.H.E.
P. O. Box 157
Stephenson, MI 49887

906-753-2209

Project/Program Description:

Youths provide caring companionship for seniors living alone and help to relieve the primary caregivers of the homebound dependent for some time each week. Teens provide in-home visits with senior citizens. The nursing home personnel and a volunteer adult provide support and supervision for the teens. Fifteen to twenty volunteers participate in the program.

Name of Project/Program:

Youth Companion Program

• •

Contact Person:

Terrie Anderson
Youth Companion Program
1501 Las Vegas Blvd. N
Las Vegas, NV 89101

702-385-5147

Project/Program Description:

Approximately 85 high school and college students volunteer to help 300 to 400 homebound elderly by grocery shopping, running errands, accompanying them for walks, cooking meals, and providing some respite care.

The minimum commitment is one hour each week over the school year. The volunteers are given two to three hours of orientation and training. Certificates are presented to the volunteers at recognition dinners and picnics. The project is funded by a decreasing ACTION grant and Catholic Community Services.

Name of Project/Program:

Center for Community Enhancement

• •

Contact Person:

Stephanie Haskell, Project Director
Center for Community Enhancement
Social Science Department, Rounds Hall
Plymouth State College
Plymouth, NH 03264

603-536-5000 Ext. 2639

Project/Program Description:

Three hundred and ten volunteers participate in 42 placement sites, friendly visiting, and special events and projects. Although the Center for Community Enhancement seeks to provide opportunities to volunteer with a wide variety of populations, the emphasis has remained on the elderly population. Aside from working with residents and staff of homes for elderly people, the center provides volunteer assistance to those elderly persons who are homebound.

The Center for Community Enhancement is in its third year of placing volunteers in community service projects. The center was funded by the federal Action program in 1989. In the first two years of operation, Plymouth State volunteers contributed more than 10,000 hours of service.

Name of Project/Program:

Community Service Program

• •

Contact Person:

Marilyn Schaeffner
Community Service Program
Westfield High School
Westfield, NJ 07090

908-789-4515

Project/Program Description:

Aside from volunteering with nursing home residents, five to ten high school students serve elderly persons in their own homes—either by being a companion or by helping with chores and errands.

Name of Project/Program:

Intergenerational Program of Princeton High School

• •

Contact Person:

Hanneke Calmon, Director
YES Intergenerational Program
Princeton High School
151 Moore Street
Princeton, NJ 08540

609-683-4480 Ext. 38

Project/Program Description:

High school and university students volunteer for 25 to 30 elderly persons by providing light housework, reading, and companionship. In another project, 60 high school and 25 university volunteers provide snow-shoveling services for 50 elderly persons.

The program has one part-time coordinator and an overall budget of $20,000. Contributions are received from local fund drives, foundations, and corporations. The Princeton High School provides an office as a contribution.

Name of Project/Program:

Summer Volunteer Service

• •

Contact Person:

Camy Condon
New Mexico Conference of Churches
124 Hermosa Street, SE
Albuquerque, NM 87108

505-255-1509

Project/Program Description:

Fifteen to forty volunteers between the ages of 12 and 16 visit 100 to 200 frail and homebound elders in different projects throughout the year. The project is sponsored by the New Mexico Conference of Churches, which maintains a statewide intergenerational network. Urban and rural projects are developed by teachers in association with the intergenerational network. Some of the projects are social studies curriculum-based and others follow the church/community model.

Name of Project/Program:

International Service Program

• •

Contact Person:

Maryann A. Rettino, CSW
Program Coordinator
Great Neck Senior Citizens' Center, Inc.
Senior Community Service Center
80 Grace Avenue
Great Neck, NY 11021

516-487-0025

Project/Program Description:

Trained and supervised teens make weekly visits to homebound elderly to bring warmth and companionship and to strengthen the bonds between the generations. The young volunteers go shopping with the seniors, share experiences, interests and hobbies, play games, pay a friendly visit, go for a walk, read or help with mail, and perform errands. Also, some nursing home visits are made.

Screening for need is done by the program coordinator. Recruitment and publicity are accomplished through school presentations and organizational referrals. Twenty volunteers participate. Awards are presented annually. The volunteers complete evaluation forms.

The program is sponsored and supported by the Great Neck Senior Center and has been in operation for six years.

Name of Project/Program:

STAR Program (Support To Aged Residents)

• •

Contact Person:

Phyllis Breland, Program Manager
STAR Program
Catholic Family Center
50 Chestnut Street
Rochester, NY 14604

716-546-7220 Ext. 678

or:

Thomas House, Research Analyst
Monroe County Office for the Aging
375 Westfall Road
Rochester, NY 14620

716-274-7800

Project/Program Description:

Young volunteers, and others, provide assistance with grocery shopping, medical transportation and prescription pick-up, banking, essential errands, and occasional chore work. Volunteers are recruited by the Catholic Family Center through volunteers' personal connections, media, community service groups, and word of mouth.

Volunteers are welcomed from all age groups, with special projects for grade school children. Internships are available. The center performs a periodic assessment of client satisfaction. A donation of $5 per service or trip is suggested.

The Catholic Family Center operates the program, which is funded by Monroe County Office for the Aging, United Way, and client contributions.

Name of Project/Program:

Friendly Visitor Program

• •

Contact Person:

Marilyn Strassberg
Tompkins County Office for the Aging
309 N. Tioga Street
Ithaca, NY 14850

607-277-0148

Project/Program Description:

The Friendly Visitor Program uses Ithaca College, Cornell University, and Syracuse University volunteers and field work students to visit homebound elderly on a weekly basis. Aside from friendly visiting, volunteers do some grocery shopping and perform small errands. Volunteers make a semester or one-year commitment.

Orientation is provided by the course instructor and staff. No stipends or fees are paid to the volunteers; however, they may receive academic credit. The program has been in existence for eight years and currently serves 30 elderly persons. Funds are received from the Older Americans Act, the state, and local sources.

Name of Project/Program:

DOROT

• •

Contact Person:

Vivian Ehrlich, Executive Director
DOROT
171 W. 85th Street
New York, NY 10024

212-769-2850

Project/Program Description:

DOROT, which means "generation" in Hebrew, is "Generations Helping Generations." Begun in 1976 when a few students delivered holiday packages to neighborhood elders, DOROT now has more than 1,200 volunteers serving 1,300 elderly persons, with 25 staff persons administering a variety of programs, including: food, housing, companionship, cultural, recreational, and educational.

DOROT's purpose is to assist Jewish homebound and homeless elderly living in New York City by (a) addressing basic needs such as food and housing, as well as health care and daily life management; (b) providing social, cultural, and educational activities to alleviate isolation and foster mutually beneficial interaction between the generations; and, (c) promoting respect for elderly persons in accordance with traditional Jewish values.

Name of Project/Program:

B'nai B'rith Hillel/Jewish Association for College Youth

• •

Contact Person:

Hanina Lassar
B'nai B'rith Hillel/
Jewish Association for College Youth
381 Park Avenue South   Suite 613
New York, NY 10016

212-696-1590

Project/Program Description:

Students from Hofstra University, Fashion Institute of Technology, Columbia University/Barnard College, Yeshiva University, Stern College, New York University, Brooklyn College, and Queens College participate in outreach activities to the homebound elderly. Activities include friendly visiting and escorting the Jewish elderly to medical appointments, community events, and special holiday celebrations.

Internships are available in which the volunteers receive a stipend and may be eligible for college credit.

Name of Project/Program:

Holy Cross High School Community Service Program

• •

Contact Person:

Michael S. Genovese
Holy Cross High School
26-20 Francis Lewis Blvd.
Flushing, NY 11358

718-886-7250 Ext. 54

Project/Program Description:

The project provides training, supervision, and evaluation of student volunteers who are helping the frail elderly homebound. Volunteers and the recipients of services are recruited through the school newsletter, local newspapers, churches, synagogues, and senior centers.

Professionals in the field of geriatrics assist the staff in sensitizing and equipping the youths to serve. Eighty-three students are serving elderly persons weekly at 18 various sites, plus visiting the homebound on a one-to-one basis upon referral from churches and synagogues.

Name of Project/Program:

Generations Joined

• •

Contact Person:

Susan Bruce, Coordinator
Intergenerational Program
Family Services of Westchester
344 East Main Street
Mount Kisco, NY 10549

914-666-8075

Project/Program Description:

High school students make weekly visits to the frail elderly and assist with errands. They serve as friendly visitors and share interests and time with elderly persons.

In recruiting volunteers, the intergenerational coordinator presents the program in the classroom and discusses with the students the issues that affect older persons. The coordinator interviews all students and the older persons to make compatible matches and, afterwards, continues to be available to both the students and the elderly persons.

Name of Project/Program:

Volunteers Serving Homebound

• •

Contact Person:

Mary Holmes Browne
Bishop Boardman Apartments
Catholic Charities
1615 Eighth Avenue
Brooklyn, NY 11215

718-965-4444

Project/Program Description:

Seniors from St. Xavier, Bishop Ford, and St. Regis High Schools volunteer to shop and provide friendly visiting. The volunteers visit two to six hours each week and receive academic credit. Close intergenerational relationships often result. Each high school evaluates its own project annually. The Volunteers Serving Homebound program is an informal effort with no outside funding or formal training. The program has been in existence for many years.

For the past 10 years, local students have also volunteered at a senior housing development to assist elderly persons. They provide escort service, shopping and social activities for approximately 60 seniors. Academic credit is given. The program does not require a minimum length of commitment. Volunteers are recruited from area churches and schools. The training is provided through tours and orientation. The program receives funding from HUD, the Community Action Committee, and the Catholic Charities Diocese.

Name of Project/Program:

Intergenerational Work-Study

• •

Contact Person:

Kevin Brabazon
New York City Department on Aging
Intergenerational Work-Study
2 LaFayette St. 15th floor
New York, NY 10007

212-577-0264

Project/Program Description:

Students receive school credits for assisting the frail elderly and helping in senior citizens centers. Students perform services for individuals (reading, shopping, friendly visiting, and delivering meals). Approximately one-third of the students receive a stipend. During a year, more than 10,000 elderly persons are assisted.

The project was started in February 1987. Currently, 14 high schools are involved. The project is sponsored by the New York City Department for the Aging, with support from the New York City public schools and private foundations and corporations. All the volunteers are at-risk students. Students are recruited who are determined to be in danger of dropping out of school because of poor attendance and/or low credit accumulation. The project has 300 volunteers with five staff persons.

Each year, a city hall ceremony is held to honor the volunteers.

Name of Project/Program:

Youth Looks at Aging

• •

Contact Person:

Ann Frazier
Extension 4-H Specialist
State 4-H Office
Box 7606
Raleigh, NC 27695-7606

919-737-3242

Project/Program Description:

4-H members decide and plan the activities that they will accomplish, including raking leaves, running errands, and visiting. A manual, Youth Looks at Aging, Leader's Guide governs the young people's activities. Some of the lessons are: You and Your Grandparent; Youth Sense: Growing Older through Music; Youth View: Aging through Pictures; and, Stories Tell About Aging.

The project has been a part of the 4-H curriculum in North Carolina for 20 years and approximately 25 counties participate. AARP sponsors the presentation of plaques as a way to recognize the work of the volunteers.

Name of Project/Program:

Franciscan University Volunteer Program

• •

Contact Person:

Sheri Spates
Franciscan University of Steubenville
Franciscan Way
Steubenville, OH 43592

614-283-6284

Project/Program Description:

Since 1986, students from the Franciscan University of Steubenville volunteer time each week with their "adopted grandparent" through the Works of Mercy program. The students provide companionship to elderly shut-ins by doing some light cleaning, chores, running errands, and occasionally taking them shopping or to the doctor's office. Visiting varies from once a day to once a week.

The project serves the Jefferson County area. Referrals are received from the County Community Action Council (CAC) and area churches. The project is co-sponsored by the CAC and the university as part of Works of Mercy program.

Name of Project/Program:

Heart-to-Heart Program

• •

Contact Person:

Debbie Liadis
Community Services Supervisor
Clearfield County Area Agency on Aging, Inc.
P. O. Box 550
Clearfield, PA 16830

814-765-2696

Project/Program Description:

Girl Scouts take valentine sunshine boxes to 225 homebound elderly during Valentine's Week. The program has been in operation for the last three years. The decorated boxes include baked goods, cards, fruit, and toiletries. The Girl Scouts visit in pairs, accompanied by adult volunteers from the senior centers. This is a once-a-year program, but it is growing each year.

Care managers at the area agency on aging and Girl Scouts refer the homebound elderly to be visited. The program is sponsored by the Clearfield County Area Agency on Aging. No costs are involved since the box contents are donated.

Name of Project/Program:

PROJECT LIVE (Living Independently through Volunteer Efforts)

• •

Contact Person:

Ruth Martin
Knoxville-Knox County Office on Aging
M.L.B. Building
Knoxville, TN 37914

615-524-2786

Project/Program Description:

PROJECT LIVE offers elderly persons help with chores and needs such as grocery shopping, filling out insurance forms, raking leaves, transportation, and reminiscing. Volunteers commit to at least three hours once a month.

Most of the volunteers are recruited from the University of Tennessee, the Johnson Bible College, and the Pellissippi State Technical Community College. Training is provided by specialists in psychology and gerontology. Except for reimbursement for mileage, no fees or stipends are paid. Approximately 80 seniors are served in Knox County. An ongoing evaluation is sponsored by the Knoxville-Knox County Community Action Committee Office on Aging.

Name of Project/Program:

South Austin Caregivers

• •

Contact Person:

Sister Madeleine Sophie Weber
South Austin Caregivers
205 E. Monroe
Austin, TX 78704

512-448-6489

Project/Program Description:

The program provides a supportive network of services to persons over 60 years old. Volunteers help residents of South Austin maintain their independence and enhance their quality of life.

Among the services provided by volunteers are rides to medical appointments, grocery stores, beauty and barber shops, library, and social service agencies; yard work; taking dogs to vets; light household tasks; minor household repairs; and visiting at home. Both younger and older volunteers participate in the project. In 1991, South Austin residents over the age of 60 received more than 700 hours of service from 70 volunteers.

The program is staffed by a community service coordinator, an associate professor of psychology at Saint Edward's University; a community church volunteer; and, each semester, five Saint Edward's University students, who receive credit in their community service courses.

Funding comes from donations by neighborhood churches and recipients of services.

Name of Project/Program:

Center For Service-Learning

• •

Contact Person:

L. Courtney Walthour
Center For Service-Learning
41 S. Prospect St.
Burlington, VT 05405

802-656-2062

Project/Program Description:

Since the mid-1970s, University of Vermont students visit elderly in their homes or nursing homes through the Adopt-A-Grandparent program—one of 11 Volunteers-in-Action programs sponsored by the center. Volunteers commit for one school year, with the hope that they will continue on beyond that time. They visit for at least two hours each week.

Approximately 35 students volunteer for the program . Volunteers are recruited through ads, flyers, announcements, and informational meetings. Some academic credit is available. The project is funded by the Center for Service Learning and by the University Student Association.

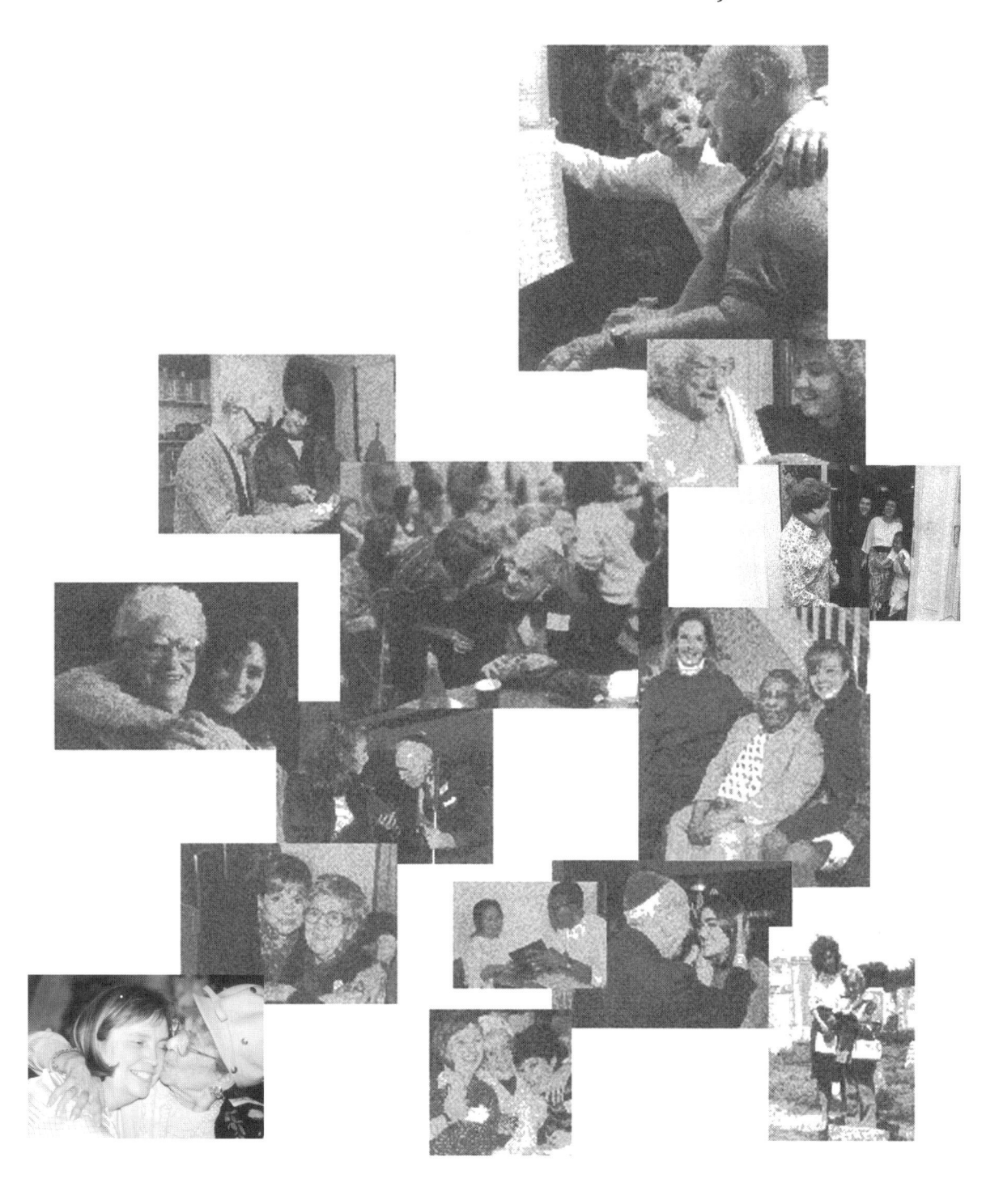

Telephone Reassurance Projects

Let Us Serve Them All Their Days • 129

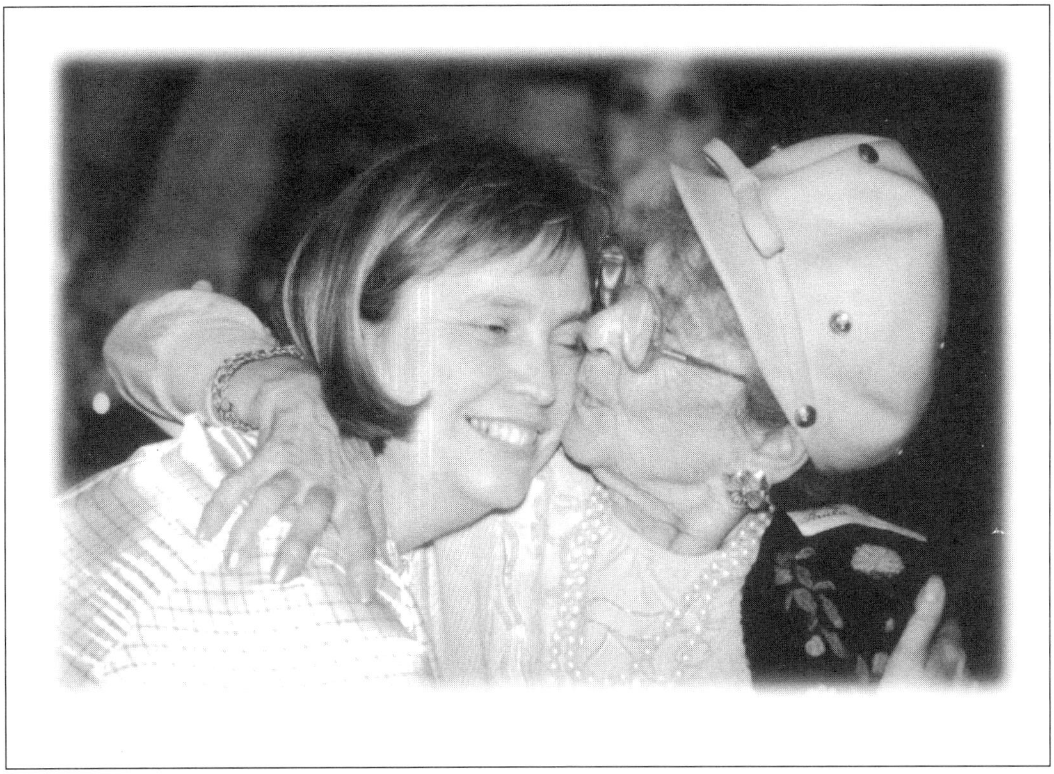

Introduction

For volunteers who would rather "let their fingers do the walking," telephone reassurance calls are a wonderful way to stay in touch with an elderly person. Making a daily reassurance call is simple and inexpensive. Students who don't have transportation available for friendly visiting are able to volunteer. In the Sheltering Arms project in Houston, Texas, students as young as 13 years old are able to participate.

Frequently telephone reassurance calls are combined with a friendly visiting or home chore project. For example, since the early 1980s, students of the University of Iowa, Iowa City, have provided telephone reassurance and, in addition, friendly visiting, food distribution, and chore service to area homebound elderly.

The calls can be simple "check up" calls to determine if the elderly person is in need of assistance. Or the calls can be structured for a more lengthy conversation, allowing the two persons to get to know each other better. Strong friendships can develop even when it's not possible for the volunteer and the elderly person to meet face-to-face and spend a lot of time together.

An expanded version of the telephone buddy call is the "telephone university" sponsored by DOROT in New York City, discussed in the section on Home Services Projects. Through a conference call, several elderly persons not only get to know a volunteer, but they can also learn more about a topic of interest and get to know each other.

Name of Project/Program:

Elderly Services

• •

Contact Person:

David Purdy
Elderly Services Agency
28 South Linn St.
Iowa City, IA 52240

319-356-5215

Project/Program Description:

University of Iowa student volunteers have provided telephone reassurance, friendly visiting, food distribution, and chore service to area homebound elderly since the early 1980s—often the result of class or social work major requirements, or service projects by fraternities and sororities. The aging studies program at the university is located near campus.

Recruitment is by word of mouth, posters, and newspaper ads on campus. Referrals are often made through visiting nurses. All services are free, except chores such as snow removal and grass cutting, which are subsidized by the Health Department. Those students who make a longer commitment have developed close friendships with seniors. The program is funded by local, county, and federal funds, United Way, and private donations.

Name of Project/Program:

Pyramid/Horizon Program

• •

Contact Person:

Jean B. Rose, Teacher
Scotia-Glenville High School
Scotia, NY 12302

518-382-1231

Project/Program Description:

Local high school students visit elderly at least twice a month in the Bridge to Friendship program. A team of four high school students, led by a 12th grader, is matched with an older person from the community who is not able to get out into the world. In groups of two to four, the students visit their elderly friend twice a month.

Through the Key Calls program, other students make daily phone calls to elderly who live alone. Every day between 7:00 a.m. and 8:00 a.m, students call members of the community who live alone. If they do not get an answer within that hour, they call the police, who go to the home and check on the resident.

The programs have been operating since 1988. Students are recruited through school announcements. As part of their training, students are given an orientation on the needs of older people. About 20 elders are served in the Bridge to Friendship program and another 20 in the Key Calls program. Although a teacher is available for support and advice, the programs are coordinated solely by the students.

Name of Project/Program:

Fordham Preparatory School Intergenerational Program

• •

Contact Person:

Kathleen Smith
Eastchester Office for the Aging
40 Mill Road
Eastchester, NY 10709

914-793-5800

Project/Program Description:

Students from Fordham Preparatory School visit once a week with at least two homebound elderly for friendly visiting and to help with chores, including grocery shopping. The volunteers also provide telephone reassurance. They commit for one school year as part of their community service requirement. Approximately 50 seniors interact with 10 college students. The project is evaluated through feedback from volunteers and the elderly persons served. Project does not receive any funds.

Name of Project/Program:

Student Telephone Buddy Program

• •

Contact Person:

Lanette Gonzales
Director of Volunteer Services
Sheltering Arms
701 North Post Oak, Suite 500
Houston, TX 77024

713-956-1888

Project/Program Description:

High school students, age 13 through 19, share friendship by phone with older persons, who may be isolated and homebound. The call is a friendly tie between the two people, a time of sharing conversations about pleasant experiences and activities.

The telephone buddies call the older persons two or three times a week at a mutually convenient time, for eight to ten-minute conversations. Weekend calls are encouraged. The recruitment of the volunteers is primarily through schools and church groups. A one-hour orientation for the telephone buddies is required.

The program is sponsored by United Way and by donations from corporations.

Name of Project/Program:

Befriend the Elderly

• •

Contact Person:

Irene Fisher, Director
Lowell Bennion Community Service Center
101 Union Building
University of Utah
Salt Lake City, UT 84112

801-581-4811

Project/Program Description:

Through the Lowell Bennion Community Service Center, students of the University of Utah volunteer to befriend elderly people with friendly visiting and weekly phone calls and to do monthly projects such as cleaning up yards and doing minor repairs. Students receive no academic credit, fees, or stipends.

The recruitment campaign is held at the beginning of the school year and after the spring break. Volunteers receive a two-day training workshop and orientation. Project directors give recognition through sending "thank you" notes and having pizza parties. Five hundred sixty-five volunteers and 28 staff persons are involved with the project. Support is received from federal grants and private donations.

OTHER SERVICE PROJECTS

Let Us Serve Them All Their Days • 137

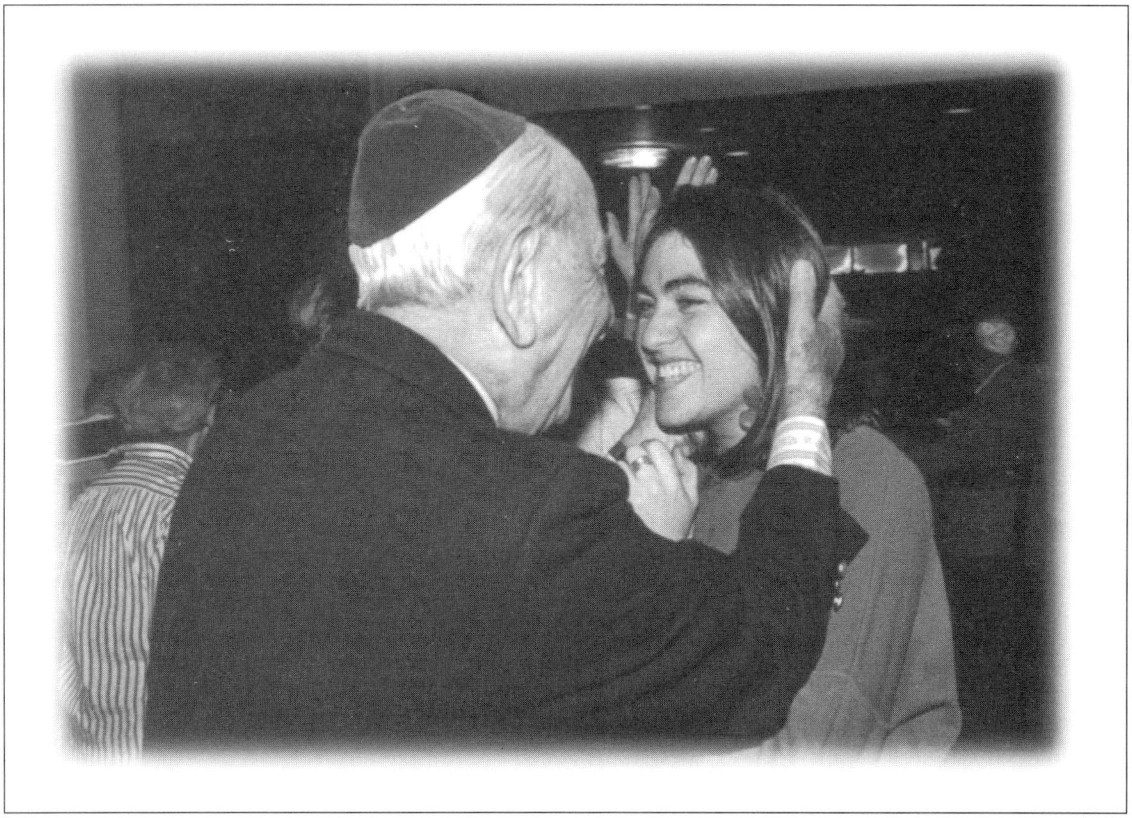

Here are projects slightly off the beaten path that we have categorized under the heading of "Other Service Projects." Included are projects that serve as clearinghouses or umbrella organizations, and projects involving community advocacy, credit hours, residence arrangements, service hours, service credits, and other innovative approaches.

If you want to know more about a particular project, call The National Council on the Aging. Or call the project directly. They will be glad to share information with you.

Name of Project/Program:

Elderserve/Homeserve/Homeshare

• •

Contact Person:

Tandy Trost, Student Coordinator
Community Service Program
14A Eisenhower Hall
Kansas State University
Manhattan, KS   66506-1009

913-532-5701

Project/Program Description:

Three separate projects are involved: Elderserve, Homeserve, and Homeshare. Elderserve addresses the needs of elderly persons in terms of the community. Elderserve community teams, composed of three students and one teacher-leader, work in Manhattan and rural Kansas areas to develop transportation projects and other community projects that affect the aged, including the improvement of facility access.

Homeserve matches residents 60 to 80 years of age who are in need of assistance on a regular basis. College students provide home maintenance, repair work, and friendly visiting. In the Homeshare project, which is now in somewhat limited operation, the student lives in an elderly person's home and receives low-cost housing in return for housekeeping services.

Commitment for the student is for one to two semesters. Recruiting is by on-campus ads, posters, and in-class presentations. The community teams receive special training in community dynamics and community relations. Few receive academic credit and fees are not paid. Recognition parties are held, and certificates and pins are awarded to the volunteer students. The program serves more than 1,000 seniors. Kansas State University helps with evaluation of the program. Support is provided by the United Methodist Ministries Fund.

Name of Project/Program:

Youth Serving Senior Centers in the Monroe Area

• •

Contact Person:

Shirley Cagle
Ouachita Council on Aging
1209 Oliver Road, Box 14363
Monroe, LA 71210

318-387-0535

Project/Program Description:

The Ouachita Council on Aging reports that the following services are performed by youth in the community:

• Approximately 10 volunteer Northeast Louisiana University students call the frail elderly homebound on the weekends.

• Harvest of Hope is a group of young people from various churches who go into the fields and pick the leftover crops, which are distributed to elderly people. Approximately 25 volunteers also deliver meals to the homebound.

• High school students provide a traditional Thanksgiving Day dinner for approximately 100 senior citizens.

• Delta Vocational School of Nursing sends six student nurses to the Carolyn Rose Strauss Senior Center in Monroe each week to provide foot care (trimming of toenails) for elderly persons.

• High school art students came to the center and painted a Christmas scene on the atrium window. St. Paul's Day School entertain at the Center at Easter and Halloween.

Name of Project/Program:

Respite Care for the Elderly

• •

Contact Person:

Sondra N. Barrios, Director
or
Barbara Payne, Respite Coordinator
LaFourche Council on Aging, Inc.
LaFourche Area Agency on Aging
P. O. Box 187
Lockport, LA 70374

504-532-2381

Project/Program Description:

Respite Care for the Elderly provides relief for caregivers. Either the caregiver, care recipient, or volunteer must be 60 years old or older. This service cannot exceed six consecutive hours for one day per week.

The volunteers benefit from the program because they know they are needed and have something of value to offer. Also, the volunteer can bank service hours for up to five years. They receive a stipend of $2.50 an hour for their service, which includes mileage.

Younger volunteers are recruited from the community trade school and Nicholls State University. The university students are frequently interested in health care professions. Older volunteers are recruited through the local RSVP Program, the eight senior centers, and the other services of the LaFourche Council on Aging, such as transportation and outreach. Local newspapers are also used for recruitment of volunteers.

The training of volunteers is handled through the Nursing Department of Nicholls State University and St. Anne General Hospital. The program has a total of 11 trained volunteers. Funding is received from the United Way for South Louisiana.

Name of Project/Program:

The Volunteer Incentive Service Credit Account Program (VISCAP)

• •

Contact Person:

William Dubord, Executive Director
or
Mary Bunnin, VISCAP Director
Community Action Agency and Human Resources Authority
507 First Avenue North
Escanaba, MI 49829-3998

906-786-7080

Project/Program Description:

A Community Action Agency, VISCAP assists the primary caregiver (the individual responsible for the care of a handicapped or disabled person or a senior citizen) in helping the care recipient remain in his or her home. To be eligible for the service, either the caregiver or care recipient must be age 60 or older.

Volunteers earn service credits—one hour of service equals one credit. The volunteer designates the person to receive the service credits. One hundred ninety-seven VISCAP volunteers are enrolled.

More than 50 youth volunteers, age 12 and up, provide services such as lawn raking, companionship, snow removal, errands, pet care, and holiday services. The holiday services include setting up Christmas trees and making cookies.

VISCAP has one full-time staff person and one part-time staff person for this project. Funding for fiscal year 1991 was $37,500, from the Michigan Office of Services to the Aging.

Name of Project/Program:

City Volunteer Corps

• •

Contact Person:

Lois Whipple
City Volunteer Service
838 Broadway (3rd floor)
New York, NY 10003

212-475-6444

Project/Program Description:

The City Volunteer Corps, the nation's largest urban youth service program, annually enrolls over 600 young people who provide 325,000 hours of service on 300 projects with city agencies and nonprofit organizations. Projects include tutoring public schoolchildren, revitalizing parks, converting vacant lots into safe play areas for children, as well as caring for elderly persons.

Intergenerational programs are under the auspices of various agencies, including Daughters of Jacob Geriatric Center, Hebrew Home for the Aged, and Isabella Geriatric Center. As part of the intergenerational program, City Volunteers provide home care, escort services, and friendly visiting.

City Volunteers, working in teams of 10-15 young people, complete several projects throughout the five boroughs. In addition to providing services, volunteers attend classes to meet their individual academic needs. Classes offered include English as a Second Language, Adult Basic Education, GED, college preparatory, and college level courses.

After a year in the Corps, volunteers are eligible for a $5,000 scholarship or a $2,500 grant.

Name of Project/Program:

Reach Out and Serve the Elderly (R.O.S.E.)

• •

Contact Person:

Mary Gardner-Smith
Volunteer Coordinator
Allegany County Office for the Aging
17 Court Street
Belmont, NY 14813

716-268-9390

Project/Program Description:

Serving Allegany County residents, this program primarily uses elderly persons to help other elderly. However, future plans are to expand the intergenerational component.

Volunteers provide reassurance, friendly visiting, tax counseling, home-delivered meals, and transportation. Some chore service is provided by local school youths who are 10 to 12 years of age.

Home visits are made to screen and assess elderly persons requesting help. Evaluation is made by monthly contact with volunteers and elderly persons served. No fees are charged for services, and few volunteers are compensated.

Recruitment is through Speakers Bureau, press releases, and ads. An annual five-hour training session is required. Volunteers are given recognition by an annual tea, birthday cards, and thank-you notes.

The program is sponsored by the State Office for the Aging, and funded by the Older Americans Act Grant 3 B funds (Federal to State).

Name of Project/Program:

Student Housing Alternative with Rural Elders (SHARE)

• •

Contact Person:

Sharon Stazetski
SHARE Coordinator
California Area Senior Center, Inc.
750 Orchard Street
California, PA 15419

412-938-3554

Project/Program Description:

Under this program, now in its fourth year, traditional and non-traditional students share living quarters (at a reduced rent) with elderly people, in exchange for services such as help with errands, light housekeeping, and mowing grass. For the older adult, shared housing can mean not only these various services, but also companionship, security, and additional income. For the university student, shared housing can mean cost savings, privacy, an alternative to long commutes, and long-lasting friendships.

Student home-sharers are recruited by the California Senior Center from the California University of Pennsylvania. They are carefully screened by a coordinator, through an interview and a five-page application. The prospective home-sharer is visited several times to see if the two parties are compatible before the match is made.

Originally funded by a $63,000 grant from the Howard Heinz Foundation in 1987, the program is now funded by California University of Pennsylvania, and coordinated by California Area Senior Center, Inc.

Many of the following may be more limited in scope and funding than the preceding projects.

Name of Project/Program:

Jesuit Volunteer Corps (JVC): Southwest

• •

Contact Person:

Therese Lederer
Central Area Director
Jesuit Volunteer Corps: Southwest
P. O. Box 23404
Oakland, CA 94623-9991

510-465-5016

Project/Program Description:

A nonprofit agency that places full-time volunteers with other social service agencies for a period of one year. In exchange for their time, energy, and commitment the volunteers receives room, board, and a small monthly stipend. A wide range of placements are available, including ones working with elderly persons.

Name of Project/Program:

Volunteer Interchange Program (VIP)

• •

Contact Person:

Jeff Jackson
Pacific Presbyterian Medical Center
Volunteer Interchange Program
225 30th Street
San Francisco, CA 94131

415-563-4321

Project/Program Description:

Through an exchange of services, the Volunteer Interchange Program (VIP) provides linkages between people of different generations. People of any age may provide services, but people who only receive services must be 60 years of age or older.

The participants earn "credit hours" for time donated in service, and they may either redeem these credits for service for themselves or transfer their credits to family members or friends in need of service. These services may include meal preparation, gardening, laundry, light cleaning, respite care, transportation, or personal care. Younger volunteers are especially encouraged to take part.

Name of Project/Program:

Teens and Seniors

• •

Contact Person:

Patty Esch
Hawkeye Valley Area Agency on Aging
404 East 4th St., P. O. Box 2576
Waterloo, IA 50704

1-800-772-2032

Project/Program Description:

Emotionally disturbed boys, 12 to 16 years old, who live in a "group home" situation, volunteer to assist in setting up fund-raising bingo events at the senior center and also assist the frail homebound elderly by raking and gardening. The boys live in a residential treatment facility for emotionally disturbed teenagers.

All contributions for services go towards maintaining the group home facility in Black Hawk County. The project fosters a relationship that serves both the boys and the elders quite well. The boys consider it a privilege to be allowed to assist elderly persons.

Name of Project/Program:

Birmingham Area Seniors Coordination Council (BASCC)

• •

Contact Person:

Carol Marsh
Birmingham Area Seniors Coordination Council
P. O. Box 12009
Birmingham, MI 48012-2009

313-642-1040

Project/Program Description:

A networking, volunteer project serves as a clearinghouse to help volunteers get in touch with those in need.

Among other volunteer services for elderly persons, BASCC connects homebound seniors who need home chores done with scout troops, Eagle Scout projects, and high school athletic teams.

Recognition awards are presented at ice cream socials. The program has been existence for 12 years and requires no funding.

Name of Project/Program:

SUNY Internship

• •

Contact Person:

Christine Sears
Madison County Office for the Aging
PO Box 250
Morrisville, NY 13408

315-684-9424

Project/Program Description:

The State University of New York (SUNY) at Morrisville sponsors an internship program where one student each semester accompanies a caseworker in friendly visiting, telephone reassurance, and respite care. The volunteer makes a six-hour commitment per week. College credit is given, with the project shown as part of the human services curriculum.

The project is administered on a volunteer basis and does not receive any funds.

Name of Project/Program:

Student Community Service Project

• •

Contact Person:

Eleanor O'Boyle, Project Director
Daphne S. Hazel, Project Coordinator
Mercy Medical Center
1000 North Village Ave.
Rockville Centre, NY 11570

516-255-2278

Project/Program Description:

The goals of the project are twofold: (1) enable high school students to learn about health careers through volunteer placements in various departments within the hospital, and (2) sensitize students to the needs of older adults and increase their awareness of the aging process through intergenerational activities and educational workshops. Approximately 45 student volunteers assist in several departments on a regular basis (such as Nursing, Lab, Finance, Older Adult Services, Pharmacy, and Admitting).

Every three months, students come together with older adults for an intergenerational sharing session. Both students and adults have expressed satisfaction and enjoyment with this program, which seeks to encourage understanding and communication between the generations. Two years ago, the Nursing Department of Mercy Medical Center received funding from ACTION to implement this project.

Name of Project/Program:

Volunteer East Tennessee State University (ETSU)

• •

Contact Person:

Sherry Russ
Coordinator, Volunteer Programs
Volunteer ETSU
East Tennessee State University
P. O. Box 70618
Johnson City, TN 37614

615-929-5675

Project/Program Description:

Volunteer ETSU serves as a clearinghouse for students interested in community service. In addition to sponsoring 10 to 12 large-scale projects each year, Volunteer ETSU continuously fills requests from local agencies needing volunteers.

In addition, several student groups on campus sponsor such programs and Volunteer ETSU recognizes and supports them. One fraternity has instituted an "adopt-a-grandparent" project and another hosts parties and dances for elderly persons.

Other Perspectives on Intergenerational Projects

Let Us Serve Them All Their Days • 153

154 • *Let Us Serve Them All Their Days*

To gain other perspectives on the identification of key elements needed for creating a project where the young assist the frail, homebound elderly, we invited four leaders in the field of intergenerational projects to offer their ideas and suggestions. The four persons were Sally Newman, Ph.D. (with James M. McCrea), University of Pittsburgh, Pittsburgh, Pennsylvania; Marvin A. Kaiser, Ph.D., Kansas State University, Manhattan, Kansas; Vivian Fenster Ehrlich, Executive Director, DOROT, Inc., New York City, New York; and Nancy Z. Henkin, Ph.D., Temple University, Philadelphia, Pennsylvania.

Dr. Sally Newman's suggestions centered on school-based volunteer projects. Among the elements needed are the following:

• Investment: The two systems (the school and the agency serving older adults) must have a vested interest and a shared commitment in the program.

• Management: Logistics (such as transportation, appropriate size of the group, size of the facility) need to be arranged in advance.

• Scheduling: Scheduling of meetings between young persons and elderly persons should be flexible.

• Planning: Program activities should be planned carefully by the leadership of both systems.

• Expectations: The staff of the agency serving the older adults and elderly persons should be oriented as to expectations of the project.

• Training: The young people should be introduced to concepts of aging such as normal aging, the frail elderly, safety, and conversation skills. In addition, expectations of the older people and staff as well as behavior and conditions should be emphasized.

• Voluntary Participation: Both the older and younger people should be reminded that their participation in the project is voluntary.

Dr. Marvin Kaiser maintains that ". . . we have a unique opportunity, given the aging of our societies, to create opportunities in which the aged can continue to use their accumulated wisdom, knowledge, and experience to serve the community and all its citizens. Such service can be of value both to the aged and to the community members. The aged are looking for opportunities to continue to be responsive, contributing members of society. And in every community there are considerable needs to be addressed but limited resources to do such.

"It is in this context that intergenerational programming has such great potential. It can provide opportunities for the aged to be of real and substantive service to the community through a range of activities which benefit the young. It also provides opportunities for the young in the community to provide practical and substantive service to the aged members of the community. And, in all cases, it provides an effective mechanism for both the old and the young to receive needed services, as well as interpersonal, emotional support.

Therefore, intergenerational programming, to be truly effective, must ensure that support and service are so structured that the giving, as well as receiving, flows in both directions. As noted above, any programming or policy that is structured to create further dependency on the part of any group, but especially the elderly, is to deny the creative potential, the energy and the emotional needs that reside within that population group."

One strategy, according to Dr. Kaiser, is to focus on a community development approach. This approach is particularly effective ". . . with the use of secondary and post-secondary students who bring planning skills to work with community-based older persons. This community development approach to intergenerational programming is particularly effective in settings where the need for planning skills is more acute, including rural areas and inner cities."

Vivian Fenster Ehrlich, Executive Director of DOROT, Inc., located in New York City, presents a perspective from the trenches. DOROT was started 16 years ago by a few university students who wanted to reach out to the frail elderly. The organization now involves hundreds of volunteers.

According to Ms. Ehrlich, DOROT's success is due to the following:

• Dual mission which considers the needs of both volunteers and the aged in all program planning;

• Many volunteer opportunities serving both individuals and groups, with different levels and time commitments;

• In-depth interviews of volunteers and elders to identify emotional, intellectual, and social needs, which are then translated into appropriate matches and activities;

• Extensive group and individual age-appropriate training for every volunteer;

• Frequent follow-up with old and young alike to ensure continuity and offer support;

• Frequent volunteer recognition such as newsletters, parties, greeting cards, gifts, awards; and

• Use of broad surveys to identify new needs and to evaluate and improve the programs.

Dr. Nancy Z. Henkin identifies five elements that are key to successful fund-raising.

Creativity

Intergenerational programming is clearly an innovative concept; most public and private granting agencies do not list it as a priority funding area. Therefore, it takes ingenuity and flexibility to fit this concept into the stated priorities of funders. Since intergenerational programming is most effective when it is used as an approach to meeting community needs, you should identify funding sources related to specific program areas such as health care, family support, community-based social services, community service, and work force readiness.

Preparation

Adequate time and staff resources to investigate possible funding sources and write solid proposals are key components of successful fund-raising. Sometimes it may be necessary to prepare a "quick and dirty" response to an Request For Proposals (RFP), although this is not the best approach. Understanding the mission and priorities of specific funding agencies and establishing personal contact with program officers is critical. Sometimes foundations will assign a program officer to an agency as a guide in proposal development. Such an inside contact can ensure that the proposal is in line with current foundation goals.

Networking

Networking with other organizations, funders, and community leaders is an important component of both project planning and fund-raising. Although you may be very interested in applying for a specific grant, your agency may not be the most appropriate grantee. Talk to large health care or social service agencies, hospitals, or schools of social work or education at local universities about submitting joint proposals. Often it is best to begin as a subcontractor for a larger agency, making the intergenerational project part of a more comprehensive program. If you are successful and develop a strong track record, you can apply on your own later.

Persuasiveness

A good fund-raiser is an effective marketer. You are "selling" a project or idea. Genuine enthusiasm and commitment must come across in face-to-face contact with program officers and in proposal writing. Try to arrange a meeting with a funding agency. If you already have a project in place and are seeking continuation funds, take an enthusiastic participant along with you to make a presentation. If you are just beginning, use existing audio-visuals or evaluation reports to underscore your points. Real life anecdotes are also valuable in helping funders visualize the impact of the project. It is important that you clearly describe how this intergenerational project will benefit both youth and elders. This "double utility" concept is very appealing to funders.

Persistence

In order to be an effective fund-raiser, you have to learn not to take rejection personally. If your proposal is not approved, call the program office and ask for feedback. Respond to the feedback and incorporate it into an updated proposal for resubmission. Never throw away a rejected proposal; it serves as the basis for a new proposal to other funding sources.

Each of these four leaders in the field of intergenerational programs identifies the crucial elements of a successful project in their own way and from their own perspectives. Whatever your particular approach, what is important is to begin. As you proceed, you will learn what works for you and for your community. The Chinese proverb says that there is no need to search for the Way, you're standing on it.

Resource Guide

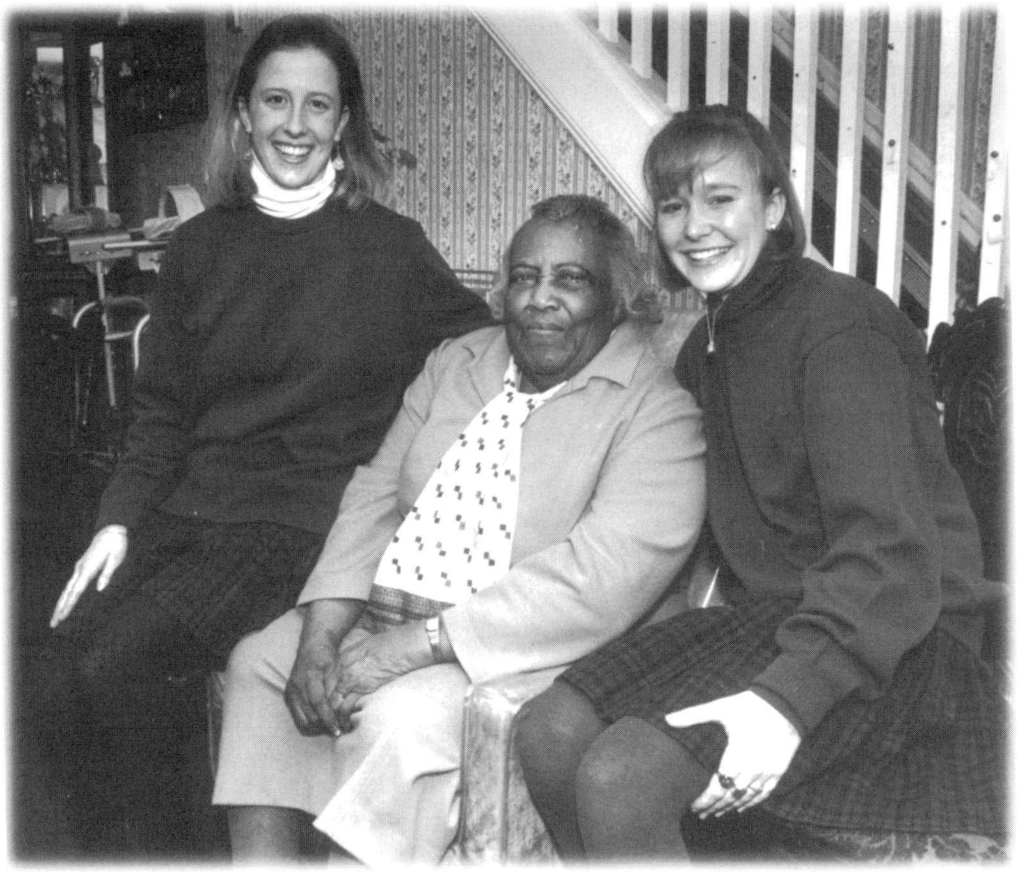

The following people have been selected because of their expertise in the field of intergenerational programs. Several have been pioneers in the field, and all are recognized for their knowledge and dedication. Although they represent diverse backgrounds and a wide variety of experiences, they share a common commitment to helping younger and older people rediscover each other.

This is a partial list. The names of all the people who are dedicating themselves to intergenerational programs would fill a book. The person who can help you in initiating or expanding a project probably lives in your community, perhaps down the road, a block away, or next door.

Nancy Blanks-Bisson, Director
Southeast Programs
Save the Children
12-1/2 Wall Street—Suite B
Asheville, North Carolina 28801
(704) 251-5204

Sheryl Boyd, Chairman for Development
Internal Medicine
Texas Tech University Health
  Sciences Center
4C103 HSC Building
Lubbock, Texas 79430
(806) 743-3161

Robert Burkhardt, Jr.
American Honda Education Corporation
1601 High Street
Boulder, Colorado 80304
(303) 442-7655

Miriam Charnow, Director
Family Friends Resource Center
National Council on the Aging, Inc.
409 Third Street SW
Washington, D.C. 20024
(202) 479-6675

Camy Condon
New Mexico Conference of Churches
124 Hermosa Street, SE
Albuquerque, New Mexico 87108
(505) 255-1509

Carol Hegeman
Director of Research
Foundation for Longterm Care
194 Washington Avenue
Albany, New York 12210
(518) 449-7873

Nancy Henkin, Ph.D., Director
Temple University Center on Intergenerational Learning
1601 N. Broad Street, Room 207
Philadelphia, Pennsylvania 19122
(215) 787-6836

Austin Heyman, Executive Director
Interages
9411 Connecticut Avenue
Kensington, Maryland 20895
(301) 949-3551

Marvin Kaiser, Ph.D., Associate Dean
Arts and Sciences
Kansas State University
Eisenhower Hall
Manhattan, Kansas 66506
(913) 532-6900

Mary Ann Levine, Director
Community Council, Inc.
Glendale Office
6010 W. Northern Avenue #102
Glendale, Arizona 85302
(602) 937-9034

Dan Leviton, Ph.D., Director
Adult Health and Development Program
  and Camp Rediscovery
HHP Building
University of Maryland
College Park, Maryland 20742
(301) 405-2588

Pauline Mahon-Stetson, Chair
Let's Link Ages in Virginia
c/o Northern Virginia Community College
3001 N. Beauregard Street
Alexandria, Virginia 22311-5097
(703) 845-6437

Claire Martin, Director
Senior Outreach
Points of Light Foundation
736 Jackson Place
Washington, D.C. 20503
(202) 408-5162

Betsey Douglas McDonald, President
Preservation Art
1128 Main Road
Westport, Massachusetts 02790
(508) 636-2929

Winifred McDuffie
Director of Volunteers and Education
Senior Neighbors of Chattanooga, Inc.
10th and Newby Streets
Chattanooga, Tennessee 37402
(615) 755-6105

Sally Newman, Ph.D., Executive Director
Generations Together
University of Pittsburgh
121 University Place #300
Pittsburgh, Pennsylvania 15260
(412) 648-7150

John Pinter, President
Easter Seal Society of Utah, Inc.
331 South Rio Grande Street
Suite 206
Salt Lake City, Utah 84101
(801) 531-0571

Deborah S. Rockman, Esq.
Program Coordinator
Legal Services for the Elderly
861 Park Avenue
Baltimore, MD 21201
(301) 3986-1322

Tess Scannell
Generations United
c/o Child Welfare League of America
440 First Street NW   Suite 310
Washington, D.C. 20001-2085
(202) 638-2952

Carol Schultz, Ph.D., Project Director
Center for the Study of Aging
University of Missouri
202 Clark Hall
Columbia, Missouri 65211
(314) 882-4851

Mark R. Sellers, Vice President
CompDrug
700 Bryden Road
Columbus, Ohio 43215
(614) 224-4506

Andrea Sherman
Intergenerational Program Specialist
16 Hellbrook Lane
Ulster Park, New York 12487
(914) 339-8321

Frank Slobig
Youth Service America
1319 "F" Street NW
Suite 900
Washington, D.C. 20004
(202) 783-8855

Maureen Statlend, Program Director
Serve our Seniors
2121 S. Goebbert Road
Arlington Heights, Illinois 60005
(708) 364-8689

Laura Sturza
The Dance Exchange
1746-B Kalorama Road NW
Washington, D.C. 20009
(202) 232-0833

Rey Tejada, Program Officer
Foster Grandparents Program
ACTION
1100 Vermont Avenue, N.W.
Suite 6100
Washington, D.C. 20525
(202) 606-4849

Carol H. Tice, M.Ed., President
Lifespan Resources, Inc.
1212 Roosevelt
Ann Arbor, Michigan 48104
(313) 994-4715

Cathy Ventura-Merkel
Senior Education Specialist
American Association of Retired Persons
601 E Street NW
Washington, D.C. 20049
(202) 434-6070

Leslie Wilkoss, Director
Membership Services
National Association of Service
 & Conservation Corps
666 Eleventh Street NW
Suite 500
Washington, D.C. 20001
(202) 737-6272

Summary

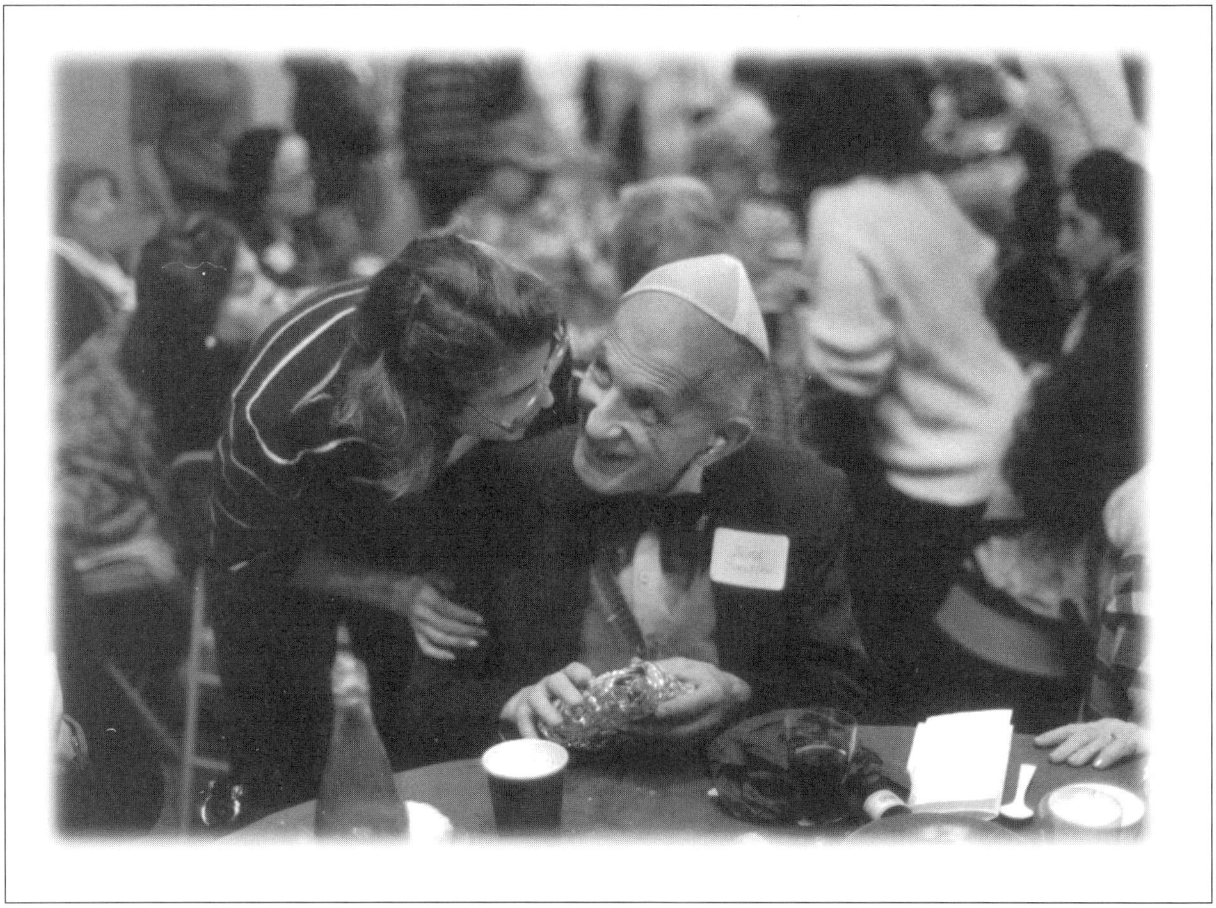

"I believe in love. It is the only possible solution. It is the only answer." This conviction was expressed by Armand Marquiset, founder of the Little Brothers—Friends of the Elderly (formerly Little Brothers of the Poor). According to Roger Nash, National Executive Director of the Little Brothers, "We find volunteers to take the place of lost friends and family, to give the loving kindness and help that is absent from their lives. And in encouraging participation by all ages, we provide a likeness of the natural family, connected to each other, through love across the generations."

The various projects discussed in this document are different expressions of the same desire—the desire to reach out to elderly persons who need our help and our friendship. And more than that, we need them. A college student said that the few hours she volunteers each week is her quiet time, the time when she is not involved in a swirl of activities, a time when she can simply be with another person.

Dr. Marvin Kaiser quotes from the Vienna International Plan of Action on Aging that "...the problem of aging today is not just one of providing protection and care, but of the involvement and participation of the elderly and the aging." Elderly persons are not a burden that we must bear, but simply ourselves grown older.

We hope that you will be encouraged to reach out to elderly persons in your community. NCOA will be glad to offer assistance. Please get in touch with us if you are interested in obtaining additional literature on intergenerational projects, or if you desire other assistance.

NCOA has several other intergenerational program publications. If you would like to learn more about these programs, please call or write:

> The National Council on the Aging
> Family Friends Resource Center
> 409 Third Street, SW
> Washington, DC 20024
>
> Telephone (202) 479-6675
> Fax (202) 479-0735

Let Us Serve Them All Their Days may be ordered from The National Council on the Aging. Make your check or money order payable to NCOA and mail to The National Council on the Aging, Inc., Dept. 5087, Washington, DC 20061-5087. Cost per copy: $15.00 including shipping and handling. Order #2051.

362.6
Couch

Couch, Larry
  Let us serve them all their days

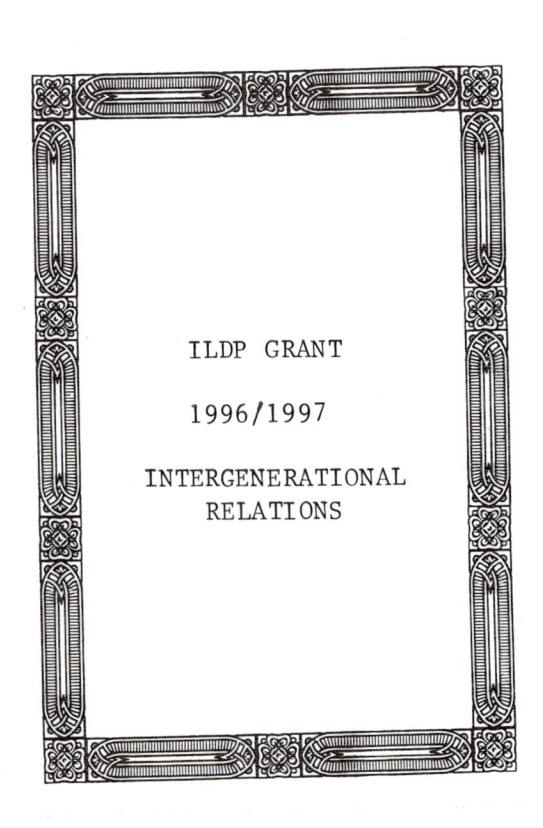

ILDP GRANT

1996/1997

INTERGENERATIONAL
RELATIONS